The Cardinal O'Hara Series

ROBERT S. PELTON · EDITOR

STUDIES

AND RESEARCH

IN CHRISTIAN

THEOLOGY

AT NOTRE DAME

The Cardinal O'Hara Series
Studies and Research in Christian Theology
at Notre Dame

Volume I

VOLUME ONE

THE CHURCH AS THE BODY OF CHRIST

K. E. Skydsgaard

Barnabas Ahern, C. P.

Walter J. Burghardt, S. J.

Bernard Cooke, S. J.

Dr. Franklin H. Littell

UNIVERSITY OF NOTRE DAME PRESS · 1963

For that portion of the book written
by Catholic theologians:

IMPRIMI POTEST: Howard J. Kenna, C.S.C.,
    Provincial

NIHIL OBSTAT: Charles J. Corcoran, C.S.C., S.T.D.,
    Censor Deputatus

IMPRIMATUR: ✠ Leo A. Pursley, D.D.
    Bishop of Fort Wayne-South Bend

    April 15, 1963

© 1963 University of Notre Dame Press, Notre Dame, Indiana
Library of Congress Catalog Card Number: 63-13473
Manufactured in the United States of America
Designed by Klaus Gemming

FOREWORD

On February 10-11, 1961, a small group of Christian theologians assembled at the University of Notre Dame to plan ecumenical discussions, which have since grown into an annual Colloquium. The purpose of this meeting is best described from the official record of the planning sessions:

The first purpose of the Notre Dame Colloquium is that Christians of differing creeds and communions, Catholic and Protestant, might sit down together to explore their respective beliefs and convictions with one another. Disagreements and cleavages are not to be winked at or set aside; indeed, it is this disparity of views which can spark irenic discussion. For the Colloquium does not aim at any conclusions or formularies of compromise. That all who follow Christ might someday be brought into one fellowship is, of course, the prayer and hope of us all. But the best approach to such a goal for the present would not *consist in any piecemeal, superficial, illusory agreements; what is called for is a deeper and more considered understanding each of the other. Too long have Catholics and Protestants relied upon third and fourth-hand accounts of what their fellow-Christians believe, too long have we entertained the false and deceptive caricature. Joined about one table at Notre Dame, in candid colloquy about theological topics and other considerations which impinge upon doctrine, dedicated Christian scholars will profit by acquaintance and knowledge, and give common witness to the contemporary world of their Christian faith—all in pursuit of God's good pleasure.*[1]

The first Colloquium held on October 6-7, 1961, had as its theme "The Theological Notion of Authority." The pattern followed was to present first of all a very orthodox and traditional notion of authority. Then a commentator upon this was to give a variant interpretation, still remaining within the mainstream of either Roman Catholicism or Protestantism. This led to deep and interesting discussion. In view of this discussion it was felt that a particularly fruitful topic for the next Colloquium would be "The Body of Christ."

"As the ecumenical council opened in Rome October 11, an ecumenical discussion between twenty some scholars, principally theologians, of various Christian faiths also began at Notre Dame, Indiana. For two and a half days members of the second annual Notre Dame Colloquium met in closed sessions to discuss papers prepared on different aspects of the central theme:

[1] Robert S. Pelton, C.S.C. "Ecumenical Perspectives—The Ecumenical Dialogue at Notre Dame," *Dialog*, II (Winter, 1963), 78.

The Church as the Body of Christ, a theme which grew out of the first Colloquium."[2]

As Father Bernard Cooke, S.J., states in his essay which appears later in this book:

No documentation would be required to substantiate the statement that Catholic theology of the Church has entered upon a new epoch in our own day; and that which is characteristic of this new period of ecclesiology is the approach to the church as mystery, as the body of Christ.[3]

After the first World War Catholic ecclesiology became less polemical and far more vital. A man who contributed greatly to this advance was Karl Adam in his book, The Spirit of Catholicism. *He was to use the Pauline symbol of the Church as the Body of Christ. In this the stress upon the Scriptural was a new emphasis within contemporary Catholic theology. The encyclical* Mystici Corporis *of Pope Pius XII, published in 1943, vindicated the stand of Adam and encouraged further developments.*

Today Catholic ecclesiology is still in growth. The biblical and patristic influences along with the confrontation with non-Roman Christian thought are proving most influential in this formation.

[2] Official news release prepared by Dr. Leonard Swidler, a Colloquium participant. Department of Public Information, University of Notre Dame, Oct. 15, 1962.
[3] Also Cf. G. Weigel, "The Present State of Catholic Ecclesiology," *Proceedings of the Society of Catholic College Teachers of Sacred Doctrine*, VII (1961), 21-31. This gives an excellent summary of contemporary developments in Catholic ecclesiology.

Concerning the first we have been provided with excellent leadership in the person of Cardinal Bea who has said:

The theologian has first of all an obligation to apprehend exactly, profoundly and from every angle the contents of the verities of Faith, such as they are contained in Holy Scripture and Tradition, and the Magisterium of the Church. He must know how to separate and determine precisely the eternal and timeless content clothed in explanations and historical formulations as the heritage of bygone centuries; when doing so, he must be careful not to weaken that content and at the same time must not give overemphasis to nonessential elements. The teacher of dogmatics must, on the other hand, face up to the problems and particular questions which arise in the present, and to the way in which such problems should be judged and resolved as an outflow of the inexhaustible treasure of the timeless and unchangeable tradition. Just as the Fathers of the Church and the great theologians of antiquity knew how to explain to the intelligence of their contemporaries the verities of the faith with the means of their epoch—think, for example, of St. Augustine, Albert the Great, St. Canisius—thus the theologian of our time must do it in an intellectual atmosphere which in many respects has undergone important changes.[4]

In regard to the second, Roman Catholics should truly be grateful to theologians of the caliber and attitude of Dr. Krister E. Skydsgaard, a Lutheran professor of systematic theology at the University of Copenhagen in Denmark. He is one of the official non-Roman ob-

[4] Aug. Cardinal Bea, "Travail scientifique et enseignement universitaire au service de l'Unité des chrétiens," *Nouvelle Revue Théologique,* 84 (1962), 2, p. 118. (Editor's translation)

servers at the Second Vatican Council, and he was a participant in the first Notre Dame Colloquium.

We first of all shall present his essay on the Church, which was prepared some years ago as a public lecture. There is no doubt that Dr. Skydsgaard has changed some of his views since that time. The Roman Catholic reader will have points of difference; but this is not the issue. It was precisely such enlightened thought which encouraged the Roman Catholic theologians, along with the wise leadership within Roman Catholicism to express more clearly and profoundly the Catholic understanding of this vital point.

This leads us into the heart of this particular study. We have three essays which show Catholic theology at work upon this subject. We present three lectures given at our 1962 Colloquium. The first approaches the theme of the Body of Christ from the Scriptural point of view. This was prepared by Father Barnabas Ahern, C.P., who is now participating in the Ecumenical Council. The Patristic understanding of this notion is given by Father Walter Burghardt, S.J., of Woodstock College, Md., and managing editor of Theological Studies. Finally, a view of a contemporary Catholic theologian is ably presented by Father Bernard Cooke, S.J., Chairman of the Department of Theology at Marquette University and former President of the Society of Catholic College Teachers of Sacred Doctrine.

Our book comes to a close with an excellent paper by Professor Franklin Littell of the Chicago Theological Seminary. He is one of the outstanding ecumenists in the United States and represents an understanding of the tradition of the Free Churches. His thesis, which can serve as invaluable aid for Catholic theological research, is that the peculiar genius of the Free Churches is not a stress upon the Church as the Body of Christ, but rather the development of the concept of the Holy Spirit continuing to inspire, move, and guide the Church *in space and time as she seeks to perceive more clearly her own nature.*

Finally, we must pay tribute to the generosity of the Archbishop of New York, Francis Cardinal Spellman, without whose help the initiation of the Cardinal O'Hara series would have been impossible.

May that same Holy Spirit continue to strongly influence such ecumenical discussions at Notre Dame and elsewhere. Under God there are now great and unique Christian opportunities for a far more profound appreciation of "the riches of Christ."

Robert S. Pelton, C.S.C., Chairman
1962 Notre Dame Colloquium

CONTENTS

Foreword *by Robert S. Pelton, C.S.C.*, Head
of the Department of Theology, University
of Notre Dame   vii

The Church

An Evangelical View of the Church *by Krister
E. Skydsgaard,* Lutheran World Federation   3

Roman Catholic Insights: A Scriptural Concept of
the Body of Christ

The Church as the Body of Christ *by Barnabas Ahern, C.P.*, Passionist Seminary, Louisville   45

Roman Catholic Insights: A Patristic Understanding of the Body of Christ

The Body of Christ: Patristic Insights *by
Walter J. Burghardt, S.J.*, Editor, Theological
Studies, Woodstock, Maryland   69

Roman Catholic Insights: A Concept of the Body
of Christ in Contemporary Roman Catholic
Theology

The Body of Christ, Catholic Theological
View *by Bernard Cooke, S.J.*, Chairman, De-
partment of Theology, Marquette University,
Milwaukee   105

Some Free Church Remarks

    Some Free Church Remarks on the Concept,
    the Body of Christ *by Franklin H. Littell,*
    Chicago Theological Seminary   127

Biographical Notes

    Colloquium Participants   141

THE CHURCH

KRISTER E. SKYDSGAARD

An Evangelical Lutheran View of
The Church

In the previous section we often met the word "church," a concept that has been very controversial since the time of the Reformation. It is closely connected with the problem of scripture and tradition. What was true then is also true now: in the question of the church the threads are gathered together but here the ways also separate. It is therefore necessary to investigate further what the word "church" contains according to Roman Catholic and Evangelical Lutheran insights.

Here also there is a common point of departure about which it is important to be clear. Both parties begin with the fact that there really is a church on earth and both proclaim their belief in "one, holy, Christian (Catholic) and Apostolic Church," as it is called in the Nicene Creed. This belief in the church is again built

upon belief in Jesus Christ as the Son of God, Lord and
Savior.

Where Jesus is only the great man, the religious genius,
the exalted moral prototype, the great proclaimer,
there can be no genuine understanding of the meaning
of church. There Jesus may have made a mighty impact
and influenced a great portion of humanity, and perhaps through his efforts may even have changed the
whole course of history. Jesus has actually accomplished all this, but that does not plumb the depths of
the secret of his nature. Jesus has not only done his
work in history as the one great outstanding personality. An association of men who hail Jesus as the great
model, as the religious genius, or as the great artist of
life, would not be a church or a congregation in the
understanding of either the Romans or the Reformers.
The church in its basic meaning exists only in that moment when there is belief in Jesus as Lord and Savior,
as the crucified, risen, and ascended one, whose mission as Lord and Savior is to be continued down
through all times, who in his spirit will constantly be
present with his saving power through word and sacrament. The church is not a collection of people who
have come together because in one way or another
they have had similar religious experiences and have
the same religious experiences and have the same religious opinions. The church is the new people which
God himself gathers and which shall reach out to all
the nations. The church is not a clique of religious people, but the church is really catholic; that is, it is appointed for all mankind, as truly as God desires to

complete his salvatory work throughout his entire creation.

Both Roman and Evangelical Christianity maintain as a completely irrelinquishible fact that the church is in existence because Jesus Christ is truly the Lord and Savior of creation who, living and present, through all ages, established his dominion on earth. God does not desire that a certain number of individuals shall be saved out of this evil world. No, God wills a *people* of men, a new humanity, through which he will lead his work in its completion. Concerning this, Roman and Evangelican Christians are agreed. But the disagreement also begins here. Let us, as in the previous section, begin by describing the Roman view of the matter.

The first, although not the most genuine impression of the Roman church, is that of a mighty institution or organization, a visible entity with a finality and a unity, with a discipline which is at the same time pliable and movable but also severe and relentless. Roman Catholics look to this institution in obedience, honor, and love; others look at it in amazement and curiosity; still others in hatred and loathing.

The institution or organization places the greatest emphasis upon the fact that it actually is a perfect earthly society, equipped with judicial and social authority, independent of any earthly state. It is a legal society with an established rule and definite ordinances which embrace all its various manifest forms and which permeate its life to the smallest details. These rules of law are collected in the so-called *Codex juris canonici*, the canonical rule lawbook with its 2414 different sections, embracing all aspects of the church's life. The church is as visible and tangible as the Kingdom of Gaul and the Republic of Venice, according to one of the great theologians of the Roman church. It can always be recognized, and very clearly be known.

Even if there be an abyss between Romanism in the various parts of the world—think for example of the difference between a primitive, superstitious, and externalized Romanism as we find it in many places in South America and that sophisticated Romanism which we meet in many places in Europe—there is still the same external unity of organization, doctrine, and cultus. There is the same priesthood with the same powers, the same episcopacy with the same apostolic authority, the same mass, to a great extent the same language in the mass and other worship, and the same faith with the same dogmas. No matter how different the setting of these things may be—and that difference may often be so great that one wonders if they are really concerned about the same things—there is nevertheless a powerful unity.

And that unity has its strongest expression in the submission to the Roman bishop, the pope. In the final analysis obedience to the pope is the decisive recognizable sign of whether one is or is not a Roman Catholic. Even if one accepts the entire body of Catholic belief, if one does not acknowledge the pope, one is nevertheless not a Roman Catholic Christian. Without relationship to the successor of Peter in the Holy See there does not exist any genuine Christianity and there is no church. And turn it about: where the pope is, there is

Christ's true and only church. He is the one and the supreme shepherd over the flock of Christ. "To be a Catholic—not only in name but also in fact—there is only one means, one alone, but this in turn is indispensable and irreparable: to obey the Church and its superior, to think as the Church and its superior." Pope Pius XI wrote in 1931 in this manner to Cardinal Schuster in Milan with respect to fascism. It is therefore necessary for us to consider for a moment the question of the pope as the successor of Peter and viceroy of Christ on earth.

The official title of the pope is: "His Holiness the Pope, Bishop of Rome, Vicar of Jesus Christ on Earth, Successor of Peter the Prince of the Apostles, Supreme Pontiff of the Universal Church, Patriarch of the West, Primate of Italy, Archbishop and Metropolitan of the Roman Church Province, and Sovereign of the Temporal Dominion of the Holy Roman Church."

When the Roman pope is legally elected and has accepted the election, he occupies with divine right the full authority of the supreme rule. No decision of any council has any binding power unless it is confirmed by the pope and proclaimed on his command. A matter that the pope has decided cannot be appealed to a general council. If it should happen that the pope should die during the meeting of a general council, the meeting or council must then be interrupted until a new pope has been elected and has decided that the meeting may be taken up again and continued. The pope has the highest and most unlimited authority in the church, and all within the church owe to him unconditional obedience, not only in matters of faith and moral questions, but in every thing that belongs to the discipline and order of the church throughout the entire world. The pope not only shares in the authority of the church but possesses it in its completeness; actually, he is that authority himself. He has not received this authority from the church—neither from a council nor from the other bishops. He has his authority solely and directly from God. His office is not conditional upon his own person or the character of his own life. No matter who he is—even if he should be an immoral person—he possesses this absolute authority in which he is absolutely and completely independent of every earthly power. "Rome has spoken; the matter is decided."

It is this authority in matters of faith and morals which was established as dogma by the Vatican council in Rome in 1870. This decision reads:

We teach and define that it is a dogma divinely revealed, that the Roman Pontiff, when he speaks *ex cathedra*, that is; when in discharge of the office of pastor and doctor of all Christians, by virtue of his supreme Apostolic authority, he defines a doctrine regarding faith or morals to be held by the Universal Church, by the divine assistance promised to him in blessed Peter, is possessed of that infallibility with which the divine Redeemer willed that his Church should be endowed for defining doctrine regarding faith or morals; and that, therefore, such definitions of the Roman Pontiff are irreformable of themselves and not from the consent of the Church.

When we evaluate this statement and try to clarify what it really contains, we must ask: What is it that causes Roman Catholicism to have bestowed upon an individual person such unlimited power and authority in the church? The Roman church justifies the bestowal of this power by referring to the position of leadership that Jesus gave to Peter among the apostles. This turns upon the famous passage in the Gospel according to Matthew (Matt. 16:18-19).

Here Jesus gave to Peter the all-embracing power and authority to rule and judge, absolute infallibility in matters of faith; in short the role of the rock in the church, without which there neither is nor can be a church. Furthermore this was not given to Peter alone but to all his successors as well. To be sure, this cannot be concluded from this biblical passage where there is no reference to anyone besides Peter, but without this understanding the text is meaningless according to the Roman reading. Later history has, after all, shown that this was the intent. Peter went to Rome and died there as the bishop, and the promise given to him is valid also to all his successors as bishops of Rome. As it is the will of God that Peter as the foremost of the apostles should have successors and as these successors of Peter obviously are the bishops of Rome, the words of Jesus to Peter also pertain with divine significance to all the bishops of Rome, all the succeeding popes.

It is not dogmatically defined but it is the common opinion of Roman theologians that it was the will of Christ that the Bishops of Rome specifically should assume Peter's position in the church, and that this was most likely also indicated to Peter by Christ himself. After the ascension of Christ, the church is not built upon Christ alone but also upon Peter who is the visible foundation of the church. Christ and his viceroy are only one head for the church. For this reason Pope

Pius XII writes in his encyclical concerning the church that those who maintain that they can worship Christ as the head of the church without acknowledging Peter as the representative of Christ find themselves in a dangerous error. It is true that Christ is the church's only Lord who has the inner invisible leadership, but Christ does not rule his church in an invisible manner, and it is through his representative on earth that he exercises a visible and divinely-instituted leadership of his mystical body. For this reason salvation is closely connected with submission to this representative.

As will be seen, there is a very close relationship between this view and the concept of tradition as we described it in the previous chapter. It can very briefly be stated in this manner: in the last analysis the pope himself represents the tradition. It is said that Pope Pius IX, who was pope at the time when the infallibility of the pope was established by the church meeting in Rome in 1870, was informed that this doctrine concerning the papacy did not have the complete support of the tradition. He is supposed to have replied: "The tradition? I am the tradition."

Whether or not this is historically true, it does cover the matter. To be sure the pope has spoken *ex cathedra* only once since that council, that is as the infallible teacher of the church, namely at the proclamation of the last Mary dogma in November, 1950. But his unique position naturally gives all his words a very significant weight and his various encyclicals also have a particularly binding power.

This power naturally reaches out first and foremost over all who are within the Roman church, but it is actually valid for all who are baptized. Also those who are baptized outside the Roman church—if the baptism is rightly administered—belong to the pope and are subject to his authority. This received a clear expression when Pope Pius IX wrote to Kaiser Wilhelm I during the *Kulturkampf* and said: "I speak in order to fulfill one of my duties which consists of speaking the truth to all, also to those who are not Catholics. For everyone who has been baptized belongs in one way or another to the Pope, which matter cannot be explained further here."

We are also told hereby how the Roman church must view other church groups. This may briefly be stated that in the eyes of God there actually does not exist any church other than the Roman Catholic. No other church can claim the name of church; all others must be considered sects.

The Roman church's view of itself has had a famous expression in the well-known sentence: "Extra ecclesiam nulla salus," ("Outside the church there is no salvation"), a sentence that has been extraordinarily discussed both outside and within the Roman church. The sentence probably originated with Cyprian, but received its sharpest elaboration in the famous bull of Boniface VIII in 1302, which reads: "We declare and decide that it is necessary for the salvation of every human that he submit himself to the Roman Pope." One of the most incisive expressions in more recent times comes from Pope Pius IX who said, "It is a pernicious error which has crept into many Catholic hearts, that one may look with assurance upon all those who do not belong to the Catholic Church. It must be maintained on the contrary as a dogma that no one can be saved outside the apostolic Roman Church and that it is the only Ark of salvation so that he who does not enter therein will perish in the great Flood." In 1864 the Pope expressed himself further that "the belief which says that someone may hope for the salvation of those who are not to be found within the true Church of Christ ought to be condemned." These would seem to be clear enough expressions that would justify those who say that according to the Roman Catholic point of view all those are lost who do not belong to the external visible church.

Actually this is not right. Directly following the first cited expression of Pope Pius IX, he adds, "Nevertheless, it ought just as surely to be maintained that they who live in ignorance of the true religion—if this ignorance is unsurmountable—are not guilty in the eyes of God." Recently in America some priests maintained that there was no salvation outside of the visible Roman church. They were emphatically disavowed by Rome which took the occasion to refresh again the Catholic teaching on this point. On the one hand it was firmly maintained that there is no salvation outside the Roman Catholic church. Only there can be found the means of grace necessary for salvation. However it is possible to belong to the Roman church without finding oneself within the jurisdiction of the church in externals. There can exist a longing even if completely unconscious within a person to belong to the church and that is sufficient if not *in re*, i.e., in external reality, then nevertheless *in voto*, i.e., according to desire and longing to belong to the Roman Catholic church. "The

Body of Christ transcends in its mystical reality the limits of the visible, organized Church," says Dominican Father Lutz in Oslo.

Those men from other church communions, or even the heathens who have no relationship with any form of Christianity, who are in good faith and by no fault of their own are in ignorance of the true faith, belong to the church by virtue of their faithfulness toward those truths which they have recognized and their innermost unconscious desire, and are therefore not without salvation. In his encyclical of 1943, Pope Pius XII cautiously states that those who do not belong to the visible fellowship of the Roman church find themselves in a situation in which they cannot be certain of their salvation. "For even if they as a consequence of an unconscious longing and desire already stand in a relationship to the Redeemer's mystical body, nevertheless they do need so many efficacious divine gifts of grace and helping means, which one can only derive benefit from as a member of the Catholic Church."

The sentence, "Outside the church there is no salvation," is thus a sentence which can be interpreted in both a broader and a narrower sense. The official position of the Roman church purports to present that sentence in its strength; but by allowing the distinction of belonging in the external, visible manner or belonging in accord with one's innermost desire, it tends to mitigate the strict interpretation. This broader interpretation is perhaps partly related to the fact that the sharper attitude toward Protestants, which were earlier spoken of as rebels and as a people who had made their belly their god, has softened and has been replaced by a more conciliatory tone. Evangelical Christians are now often spoken of as "our separated brothers" or "our Protestant brothers." A similar development has also taken place within the Evangelical church.

If such a rather far-reaching tolerance does exist for those who guiltlessly do not belong to the visible Catholic church, there is in contrast a great rigidity toward those who stand within the church. No valid ground can ever be given for doubting the Roman church and its truth, at any rate not among Catholics who have received the proper education in the truths of the faith. If someone should fall into doubt, there must be moral defects that are to blame. To give up the Catholic faith and step over into another Christian fellowship cannot be morally justified. Coercive measures toward persons are justified in case of defection or heresy. Religious freedom as such is not a good thing, and it is not good when a Catholic state relinquishes the unity of faith. One nation, one religion.

Have we then with all this sufficiently described the Roman conception of the church? Actually, no, for we have so far only considered one side of the matter. We have viewed the church as an external, legal institution, as a monarchical state with the pope at its head and with bishops as shepherds and superintendents with apostolic authority, who have been established as successors of the apostles by the Holy Spirit. We have as yet only been occupied with the external aspects of the church which after all is only one side of the picture. Protestants are often tempted to stop here and allow their judgment to fall on the basis of that which has thus far been presented.

We can get an interesting insight into the Roman concept of the church by taking a look at church history. (The following has been borrowed from a Roman theologian.)

The various epochs of history have developed different sides to the character of the Roman Catholic church. One can very well speak of transformations or changes in the concept of the church as conditioned by historical circumstances, if one is sure to make it clear that this does not mean real change, but a development in which that which previously existed preserves its truth.

In the early church, the church was the new people of God who were rescued out of this evil world and who awaited the second coming of the Lord in the very near future. It did not recognize any responsibility to permeate society but rather sought to remain outside of the worldly life as much as possible. Everything was still in many ways completely undeveloped. The Roman bishop had not yet asserted his absolute lordship in the church. There were bishops who denied that there resided any particular authority in the bishop of Rome. The Christians knew themselves as the body of Christ, as his bride, as a people that belong to him and whose head was the risen Christ himself. The various organs of the body were the functional servants necessary for the edification of the body and its fulfilment. Separation from the world had as its counterpart a fervent brotherly love. Christians were hated for the most part by the contemporary heathen world and were more inclined toward the coming than the present world.

But the Lord did not come. Consequently the barriers against the world fell. After the "liberating deed" of Emperor Constantine made Christianity into the religion of the state, Christians were forced to turn toward the world and to seek to permeate the wordly orders with Christian ideas. Later, in the midst of the collapse of Rome, the church showed itself to be the rescuing power and at the same time became the educator of the young Germanic peoples. In brief, the church began to show itself in all its secular power.

This conception of the church received historical-philosophical elaboration in the grandiose view of Augustine: The church as God's state on earth. Here begins the dream of the Middle Ages; the church as the visible kingdom of God here on earth, anchored in agreement between the spiritual and secular rulers and in which all human activity and all worldly conditions were to be formed and influenced by the Christian faith and submissive to divine law. The Roman bishop stands at the head of this City of God. He has the supreme power and possesses both the secular and the spiritual sword.

Outwardly, the church of the Middle Ages was the great power church, to which the powers of this world were forced to submit. To a great extent, the pope and the bishops entered into political activity and themselves became powers in the world. This universal, creative and powerful concept of the church had its own legitimacy but also its obvious dangers. For this reason the church had to develop further in order to give expression to other sides of the nature of the church. Not that the view of the Middle Ages is to be forgotten. On the contrary, it constantly stands as an essential link in the Roman understanding of the church. Among other things, it lies behind the phenomenon that we know today as "political Catholicism."

With the close of the Middle Ages, the Roman church entered upon a new phase which again changed the face of the church.

Now the Roman church was no longer the only church but was surrounded by churches who also made claims to be the church of Jesus Christ. In many ways the Roman church was under indictment and forced to battle for its very existence. This struggle in which it constantly claimed to be the only saving church in contrast to all the "sham churches" gave to it a narrow, often arrogant, and unsympathetic stamp that caused the opposition and distrust of the non-Roman Christian. The proud church of the Middle Ages became—to put it sharply—"The Church of the ghetto." It became a church whose legalistic nature was emphasized; the anti-Protestant polemic became characteristic of the face of the church. The church of modern times became to a greater and greater degree a church of authority, a church of dogma, wherein the pope time after time was called upon to condemn and to instruct.

In this period when the church had to appear again and again as the instructor and disciplinarian, the church's own children inevitably came to feel themselves restrained. There rose a rift between the lay people and the hierarchy of the church, who alone had the rule. This resulted in the word "church" bringing to the minds of most Catholics a concept of authority and power, and they themselves no longer experienced being a church. When catechisms came to the explanation of the church, they presented it in terms of judicial power and infallible doctrine.

The church in this period, from the Council of Trent to the present day, may therefore be seen essentially as the church of the pope with a strong, centralized rule. Never before has the pope had such great significance and influence. This received its clearest expression at the Vatican Council of 1870 when the dogma of papal infallibility was adopted.

Nevertheless this development was not without its drawbacks. It was accompanied by an incapacitation and crippling of laymen, and even of the bishops and priests. Much initiative was smothered and the distance between the church and the world grew steadily larger.

A peculiar feature of our time is that this concept of the church is also going into the melting pot. The development we are witnessing in our day is of a double nature. In part, there is a trend toward amazing independence on the part of the lay people, to a renewal of the idea of the common priesthood of the baptized, a ferment which is still in its nascent state. Everyone who knows a little bit about what the phrase "Catholic Action" contains, understands something of what is taking place here. In part, there is a trend toward a new understanding of the inner mystical nature of the church that focuses itself upon the church as the "body of Christ." In this there is a return to the New Testament and apostolic concept of the church and often a rather strong criticism of the view of the church of earlier times.

It is noteworthy that in the midst of World War II, Pope Pius XII found reason to send out an encyclical with the title: *Mystici Corporis Christi* ("Concerning the Mystical Body of Christ," June 29, 1943). Now the Pope sought to define the nature of the church clearly and plainly by returning to a biblical concept. What is the principal point of this papal encyclical? Of course, the Roman church is upheld as the only legal and true church, where the pope as the viceroy of Christ has final authority; and the pope takes the occasion seriously to warn those who in blind, reformatory zeal overstep the boundaries of a sound understanding of this point. But the main concern is nevertheless the description of the church as a spiritual organism, wherein Christ in a mystical manner works incessantly, infusing his sanctifying grace into the individual members through the sacraments. Jesus Christ contains all supernatural gifts in all their abundance and perfection. By way of the church and its means of grace these stream from him to mankind and sanctify mankind. Even as the church could never exist without its head, neither could Christ exist without his body. The body can actually be called the consummation and completeness of Christ.

The church has its external aspects—all the functions through which the truth is proclaimed and grace conferred. This may be called the bodily aspect of the church. But just as the humanity of Christ was a means of his divine nature, so is the church's external body of outer things, functions, and persons an instrument through which the divine life is transmitted to men. The church's bodily aspect is the continuation of the human nature of Christ. The church is the second Christ, the Christ himself who continues his life here on earth, mystically bound to his body through the holy functions of the church executed by those persons consecrated for that purpose. We have herewith reached the final stratum of the Roman understanding of the church: the church as the mystical body of Christ, as the supernatural and sacramental organism of salvation in which Christ is intimately and inseparably bound to his faithful and they to him.

In the following account of the Evangelical view of the church, it must first of all be noted that we are emerging from a period of the history of the Evangelical church in which there has been a very weak consciousness of what it is to be a church. Of course, this has not been true everywhere, but it is nevertheless true to a considerable degree as we consider Protestantism in its entirety. About the turn of the century, Adolf V. Harnack, who was probably the most significant Protestant historian and theologian at that time, gave a series of lectures at the University of Berlin concerning "What Is Christianity?" In these lectures he described what Christianity was without seriously entering into the concept of the church. The theme was that Christianity was chiefly to be regarded, as an individualistic relationship to God. The church had significance only of second or third rank and did not belong to that which was essential.

The famous theologian, Wilhelm Hermann, at one time visited the University of Uppsala. Here he met the man later to become so well known as professor and bishop, Gustaf Aulén, who at this very time was working on his disputation on Luther's conception of the church. When Hermann heard of this, he is reported to have said: "I congratulate Swedish theology that it has so much time and peace that it can occupy itself with something so peripheral." This view made itself felt far beyond theological circles.

Many Evangelical Christians would have been lost for an answer had they been asked what the church really was or what it meant to them. There may be various appraisals of this, as there are various views of these matters, but there can hardly be any doubt that this attitude toward the church was a fruit—many will add, a bitter fruit—of the age of enlightenment with its in- dividualism, and its tendency to change and dis- solve the biblical, reformation understanding of Chris- tianity.

In the meantime a great change has taken place on this very point in our time. The question of the church has again become living and actual. In part, exegetical re- search has led to a renewed understanding of the sig- nificance of the church in the primitive church as we find it in the New Testament; and in part, the times themselves have led to renewed questions concerning the church and the fellowship of the church. A Roman theologian wrote some years ago, "He who today asks about Christianity, is asking about the church." This is also true to a large extent in the Evangelical camp. "To have a church, a mother, which from youth could lead my steps, became the thirst and longing of my life," said the Dutch statesman and theologian, Abraham Kuyper.

It has been said in the meantime from the Roman side that the viewpoint of the Reformers was that God spoke his word to the individual man in some mystical manner that was completely independent of external means and independent of any community with other men. The Reformers were said to be basically consistent individualists. This is completely incorrect. For the Reformers also, God has related his word to a church, a community of men, to very definite, external words, to specific deeds. The fellowship of the church and its "signs," both the preaching of the word and the administration of the sacraments, precede the faith of the individual and are the means through which God encounters the individual. Modern individualism with its contempt for externals and its lack of understanding of community with others and therewith of the essential content of the word "church" does not stem from the Reformers but has other roots. The church is not for the Reformers any more than for the Roman Catholics something incidental, minor, and unessential. It is rather something basic, not only as a means, but something that indissolubly belongs to God's work of salvation.

For this reason Luther calls the church our "mother," which gives us birth and nurtures us, without which we could not even become Christians and come to

Christ as our Lord and Savior. And it was Calvin who gave expression to these beautiful words, "We may learn from the title of *mother,* how useful and even necessary it is for us to know her; since there is no other way of entrance into life, unless we are conceived by her, born of her, nourished at her breast, and continually preserved under her care and government till we are divested of this mortal flesh and become like the angels. For our frailty does not allow us to depart from this school but in our entire life we must be its disciple. Even more: outside of her lap there can be no hope for the remission of sins."

When the Reformers felt themselves compelled to leave the great church, it was not in any case because they denied or were indifferent toward the fact of the church. The question debated by Roman and Evangelical Christians is not whether or not there shall be a church but what this church is. Because the question of the true church occupied the Reformers both day and night they finally came to a break with the mighty Roman church. It was not because the Reformers were rebels who wished to split and divide at any price. Just the opposite. It was rather because, compelled in their conscience, they desired to be servants of the true church. They knew that it is not possible for men to present themselves before God as the pure church, but rather it is God who in his loving kindness constantly renews his church. That is, it was not they who were to build the new church. The church had always been. But they knew themselves compelled to place themselves at the disposal of that renewal which they saw to be necessary.

It will be necessary as a beginning to consider the Evangelical interpretation of that important passage in the Gospel according to Matthew (Matt. 16:18) on which the Roman church bases its view of the church: "And I tell you, you are Peter, and on this rock I will build my church, and the powers of death shall not prevail against it."

The disagreement concerning the meaning of this passage did not arise either yesterday or the day before, but has existed since at least the beginning of the third century. In the first two centuries we find only vague reference to the passage in Christian literature—actually it was not cited in its entirety during this period—and the church fathers who do treat the passage understand it in very divergent ways. Tertullian regards this word as one that pertains to Peter only and dissociates himself from the view that it is relevant to the bishops of Rome. Cyprian thinks of it as relevant to all bishops. Peter is on the same plane in his office and his authority as the other bishops and has no rank superior to theirs. Peter is always the sign of the unity of the church, but it is the bishops in their entirety who constitute that unity.

Origen stands quite alone in his interpretation. He spiritualizes the entire passage and finds in the person of Peter not only the apostle but "every Peter"—i.e., that this is true of all believing and confessing followers of Christ. Origen rejects the thought that the church shall be built solely and only on Peter, as Peter has no precedence over all the others who believe and confess. The passage thus speaks of all believers.

Eusebius of Caesarea interprets Christ to be the rock

and in a wider sense sees Peter as the rock, the one who confesses that Jesus is the Christ, Son of the living God. Chrysostom says of this passage, "You are Christ, and on this rock I will build my Church, that is to say: on that faith which you have confessed." But because Peter is the first of all the disciples to make this confession and is for that reason the first to go into the church, he does deserve a certain place of honor. He became the most prominent apostle and the founder of the church.

Nor does the Western church of the first three centuries have a unanimous interpretation of the passage. Bishop Ambrose of Milan does not speak of Peter as the foundation of the church. He strongly underscores the significance of Peter's faith, and it is as a man of faith that he has greater authority for teaching than the other apostles. It is in this respect, and not as one who governs and is given jurisdiction, that Rome has inherited Peter's charge.

It is naturally important to observe what Augustine found in the passage. He knew that its interpretation was difficult and had two understandings of it himself. For some it was Peter who was the rock, for others, Christ; and it was this last conception toward which Augustine leaned. "For it does not say: You are *the rock,* but you are Peter. The rock was Christ whom Peter confessed—as the entire church also confesses him—and by whom he was called Peter." It was Peter who received his name from the rock and not the rock which receives its name from Peter. When Jesus said that "upon this rock I will build my church," it means "upon that rock on which Peter has just confessed his faith." Peter himself is built upon that rock. But at the same time Peter is the living symbol, the archetype of the entire church.

Augustine knew that the choice could be difficult enough to make and allowed the reader himself to determine which of the two interpretations was correct. He did not give an authoritative explanation. However Augustine's vacillation on this did not hinder him from assigning a precedence to Peter even as the Roman bishopric was also given a rank above the others.

Later in the fifth century, however, the matter became much clearer for the Western church. At any rate since Leo I (d. 461) this Matthean passage was considered, as a matter of course, to concern in part Peter and in part his successors upon the bishop's seat in Rome. In the meantime the Eastern church went its own way, and the Greek Orthodox church today does not recognize the primacy of Peter to be valid for the Roman bishops. The rock is understood to be Christ himself; or it is the faith of Peter in Christ. Where Peter is regarded as the rock, he has only a limited personal precedence as the most prominent apostle.

These broad references are sufficient to indicate that there is by no means unanimity with respect to the understanding of this passage from Matthew. On the contrary, divergent interpretations have existed ever since the early church. The Reformers are not simply telling fairy tales in their exposition of the passage but have many predecessors in the ancient church.

Luther regards the rock as Christ. This rock is the Son of God, Jesus Christ alone, and none other. You are the man of the rock, Jesus says to Peter, for you have confessed and proclaimed the true man who is the true rock such as the Scriptures designate him, namely Christ. Peter is the rock because he stands upon the rock and thereby becomes of rock himself. In and of himself Peter is everything but a rock, as the immediately succeeding verses clearly show. "Therefore Christ allowed Peter to fall, that we might not regard him as the rock and build upon him. For we must have our foundation upon him who can stand against all devils, and that is Christ."

Calvin says that this passage deals with Peter's faith in Christ. The faith which confesses that Jesus is the Christ—which confesses together with and according to the example of the apostle Peter—is the rock on which the church is to be built.

A unique and interesting solution is proposed by a scholar who translates the text back into Aramaic, the mother tongue of Jesus, and thereby arrives at the following text: "I say unto you, yes, you, Peter, that upon this rock (namely Christ, the Son of the living God) I will build my church." In recent Protestantism there are many who have gone a completely different way and have declared that the word does not originate from Christ himself but is added later at a time and place where it was desirable to promote the person of Peter. It is very improbable that these words are from the mouth of Jesus. I do not intend to enter this discussion further. It only gives one more indication of how little certainty there is if one is to take a stand solely and completely on historical grounds. Here we will allow the words to stand as they are, and try to understand them within their context.

In the following I shall briefly consider Oscar Cullmann's book, *Peter: Disciple-Apostle-Martyr*,[1] a recent investigation of this question on Protestant
grounds. It is interesting because it treats the question
archeologically, exegetically, and dogmatically, and not
least because Cullmann in many ways agrees with the
Roman exegesis without however drawing the same
conclusions. The book has attracted much attention in
Roman as well as Protestant theological circles.

Even if Cullmann doubts that these words were spoken
on the same occasion that Matthew's Gospel records,
he is in no doubt that we do meet here a genuine word
of Christ. Nor is he in doubt that the word is spoken
directly to Peter and pertains to him personally. Here
he accordingly diverges from the interpretation of the
Reformers. The word is directed toward the *apostle*
Peter and implies all that power with which an apostle
is provided and which no one can later receive. We find
in a unique way a foundation, a word that indicates a
cornerstone. Peter is that rock upon which the entire
church is later to be built. The rock lies as a foundation;
it is something "once and for all," something that lies
firmly and plays a role that cannot be transferred to
anything else. Those who followed after could be and
were exceedingly important: deacons, presbyters, bishops, prophets, teachers, and shepherds; but they were
certainly not the foundation, not apostles, who filled a
very special place as the ones personally chosen by
Christ. It was exactly those who took this word unto
themselves who were unfaithful to that to which they

[1] Translated from the German by Floyd V. Filson (Philadelphia:
Westminster Press, 1953).

were called, namely to build upon the only foundation that existed. At this moment this was Peter, the confessing one, the apostle, the chosen one. All those who followed had only to see that the foundation, the rock, lay secure and immovable there where Christ had laid it.

We note how the whole question of scripture and tradition discussed in the previous chapter also enters here. If we are to ask how, according to this understanding, Peter can be the basis of the church through all later ages, the answer must be: that all subsequent church ages must build on the basis which is Peter. That is, to be solid and unswerving in faithfulness to his witness to Christ as it is testified to in the creed and scripture. At that moment Peter stood as the representative for that faith in Christ upon which all depends. Aside from this basis there is no rock but only sand. In this way Peter and the other apostles bore the responsibility for building the church.

The Evangelical view, as Cullmann represents it, makes a case for the apostolicity of the church equal to that of the Roman church. For him, apostolicity means: built upon Peter as the first apostle, who confessed Jesus as the Christ, the Son of the living God; not upon a chance person or an arbitrary observer, e.g., a Roman historian or a modern historian of religion. It is built on the very apostle who was a man of personal weakness—as the following account in the Gospel according to Matthew so clearly indicates—but who nevertheless by God's own revelation makes that confession upon which all depends: "You are Christ, the Son of the living God." The very cornerstone is Christ, himself. The foundation is the apostles, because they were chosen to be his witnesses, and upon their witness the church was built and must be built as long as there is a church upon the earth. The church which would continue to build, must only continue faithful to that foundation, the confessing apostle and that church in which he had the leadership.

The leadership which was given to Peter and to the other apostles must also continue in the church, not in an external, mechanical manner—Christ had given no command to that effect—but in such a way that Peter becomes the original model for all leadership. The church is truly given the power to proclaim with authority, to declare the forgiveness of sins, and where man will not hear the call to repentance, to refuse it. There is a "power of the keys" in the church. Jesus gave the authority of leadership to Peter for that early period in which the foundations were laid, but did not at all imply that the same authority would belong to specific men—namely, the bishops of Rome—after the time of Peter. There is not the slightest hint of such intent in the text itself or in the oldest tradition. It is a decisive difficulty from an Evangelical point of view that there is no support in biblical texts for one of the most important of all the doctrines of the Roman Catholic church—that only that church which acknowledges the Roman bishop is the one and true church of Jesus Christ. Even if it should be the case that Peter later came to Rome and died there, which Cullmann is historian does not find sufficient evidence to deny, there is by no means sufficient ground to guarantee such an extraordinary and extensive conclusion.

To base the Roman Catholic theory of the church, with its enormously far-reaching consequences, upon a passage of scripture like this is placing altogether too great a strain upon this text, especially since the claim cannot plead the support of early tradition. The Evangelical view must say "no" to this interpretation, which on the basis of this passage makes it possible to assign such power and authority to the bishop in Rome as no other man has ever had before or since. This is a disastrous confusion of foundation and structure. It is a historic fact that the Roman bishop, the pope, has had great importance and to a degree still has it. Evangelicals must recognize this and ascribe to that office its proper significance. But Evangelicals cannot agree that the Roman bishops are the fundamental basis and mainstay of the church of Christ on earth through all ages and that this is versified not humanly or historically, but with unqualified divine right. Here there is an "either-or."

This is arrived at on purely historical grounds as these have been developed above. Not a few Roman theologians do grant a measure of concession today—that to be sure one cannot conclusively prove the position of the Roman bishop by this passage to Matthew—but the essential fact is that Rome with its bishops actually did, in the course of history, receive the leadership of the church. Therefore one may return to this text with the conclusion that even if history is opaque, there can be no doubt that Matthew 16:18 was also relevant to the successors of Peter. This was the will of God for his church. Otherwise God must have provided poorly for it.

There are those Roman theologians who go a step further and maintain that the decisive fact is not at all whether Peter was ever in Rome or not. In the final analysis that is more a question that belongs in the realm of faith than of history. The fact that the Roman bishop is the successor of Peter with all that power which was bestowed upon Peter is of primary importance and a concept that we know to be a major link in the Roman faith. It is something that is to be believed by virtue of revelation.

Logically, we are confronted by a strange circular argument: the Roman bishop is the successor of Peter, and the viceroy of Christ is maintained through faith with tradition as the source of the revelation. In the light of this later tradition the passage in Matthew 16 is to be interpreted. But that tradition is a source of the revelation, should be verified by history, i.e., by the scripture passage in Matthew and by the oldest apostolic tradition.

The conclusion of these considerations must be that, in the last analysis, historical research is not the basis on which one decides whether or not to hold the Roman view. This depends upon deeper matters and other considerations. According to the Roman point of view, this question, as other questions of faith, can only be solved when divine grace intervenes and enlightens human minds.

An essential point in these considerations is certainly found in the fact that only through the Roman way of thinking can men be sure of their faith. Otherwise everything collapses. The guarantee—to use an expression which is perhaps too heavy-handed for the Roman

Catholic but which I use for the sake of clarity—for the truth of Christianity can only be given through this certainty in the infallibility of the church, concentrated on the person of the pope as the successor of Peter and as the viceroy of Christ. The true apostolic witness is found *eo ipso* where the pope and the bishops are, as something given beforehand. There is the truth of Christ, and there is Christ himself. Jesus has issued, so to speak, a "blank check" to Peter which reads that wherever the Roman pope may be, there truth is to be found for all time.

It must clearly be noted that the Evangelical church does not have this guarantee. It stands far less protected, much more naked and unguaranteed. There is much less to see, much less that is tangible, without any apparent external support. It must be conceded that there is very little here to take hold of. But the strange thing is that the Evangelical view, particularly where it burst out in strength and power, always stood unguaranteed and unprotected and did not make its way because it first had to prove its reasonableness or gain the religious support of man. Where the word broke through, it did not need any external support or guarantee. It was Christ himself who stood behind it.

Wherever the Evangelical view is genuine and does not succumb to the temptation to seek external guarantees and props, there is a certain distinct distrust of external supports, of a constructed, tangible system of guarantees. It is as if the word's own original power loses its authority and conviction by this strange direct identification of the human and the divine. Pope Pius XII wrote in an encyclical that, after the ascension of Christ, the church no longer builds upon Christ alone but also on Peter as the viceroy of Christ on earth, and that these two now constitute one head (as is also expressed by Boniface VIII, the pope who more than any other during the Middle Ages made the claim for the absolute power of the pope). Evangelicals deny that this is a true view of the lordship of Christ in the church. It was this very view that aroused the Reformers and led them to make their harsh judgment on the pope, even to make the accusation that he was the Antichrist—not of course in his person, but as representative of the institution which laid claim to divine authority.

The Evangelicals ask the mighty institution of the Roman Catholic church if the lordship of Christ is not hereby confused with the lordship of the Roman Catholic church and if it does not thereby identify itself with Christ and make itself independent in its relationship to Christ. Such an infallible church, according to the Roman understanding, is secured by divine supports and guarantees, in which Christ and the Holy Spirit have become one with the immanent life of the church. As the judicial, authoritative and supernatural church of grace it *is* the onliving Christ and is therefore according to the Evangelical conviction, no longer completely and essentially depending on Christ as its only Lord. That is not to say of course that Christ in his freedom and grace does not make himself Lord in the Roman Catholic church. That question is not raised here. We are concerned with the principle itself, the theological understanding of the nature of the church.

It is conceded that Romans will have a great deal of difficulty in understanding this question, which to most of them will certainly appear to be both awkward and unreasonable. Nevertheless the question must be asked: Has not Christ here been identified with a definite, earthly, human church and its power and extension? Has not Christ here been identified with the church as a religious organization? And therefore He is no longer Lord?

Here we face the most serious and profound problem of the church—that which spiritually sensitive readers catch a glimpse of in a harrowing manner in Dostoevsky's story of the Grand Inquisitor in the novel *The Brothers Karamazov*. He who is unaffected by the indictment of this story can hardly sense the problem of the church and its temptation. But we must add in the same breath that this question directs itself to both the Roman and the Evangelical church, even to every church upon the earth. Every church meets the temptation of establishing itself as a religious bloc, perhaps provided with great wordly power and influence, as a power of social influence, as an apparatus of piety and an organ of grace, as a servant of the inner religiosity of all men.

In the midst of all this the church may be an utterly apostate church, no longer an implement for the coming of God's Kingdom or for the salvatory power of Christ, but a tool of the great apostasy, the spirit of the world. Such a church would more than gladly clothe itself in the garb of religion or, even better, in Christianity, in order all the more anonymously to fulfill the mission of apostasy among the peoples of the world. The church which does not hear this question but protects itself behind some claim of divine security, perhaps in the refuge of its own native piety and sanctity, is in danger of becoming a church of apostasy. And this is true no matter what the church is called— Roman Catholic or Evangelical Lutheran. No fine theory as such, Roman or Evangelical, can help a church here. For that reason every church must turn back to the prayer that Christ may assume sovereign lordship.

Luther energetically maintains that God's church is rule by the Holy Spirit himself, that Christ is with his church on earth until the end of the world. For this reason we pray daily in our confession of faith: "We believe in one holy, catholic (universal) church." But Luther bases his belief in the church not upon a visible church with an infallible leadership, but upon Christ alone. Christ in his free grace will constantly come and through his word and holy sacraments establish his rule upon the earth. "Ecclesia semper reformanda est," said one of the theologians of the Reformation period. "The Church must constantly undergo reform." This must be true without restriction for all ages. This does not mean a reformation which is such a ceaseless merry-go-round that finally no one knows what is up or down—that would be a shocking caricature of re-formation—but a reformation in which the church always openly listens to God's word in his revelation. That word can never be identified with the church it-self but is always absolutely superior to the church and always battles against the church for the church.

"It is after all not we who can uphold the church, nor

was it our predecessors, nor will it be our successors,"
says Luther, "but it was, it is, and it always will be He
who says: I am with you always even to the end of the
age, Jesus Christ."

When access to a church meeting at Augsburg was
denied Luther, he wrote a letter to Melanchthon who
was representing the cause of the Evangelicals. In a
moment of discouragement, and pressed by over-
whelming difficulties and great opposition, Melanchthon had expressed a doubt in the cause of the Reformation. Luther then wrote to him to this effect:
"You say that you do not know where it will lead to.
But I wish to say that if our cause is dependent upon
your rhetoric or upon anything else that is human,
then I will have nothing to do with bringing it about.
Our cause belongs to only one thing, namely the faith.
And faith is this: to place one's cause exclusively in
God." In this faith alone that God both can and will
lead his cause to victory, that he will allow his word
to be heard—that word which has never been bound
by any human power—that he will provide for his
church until the end of time, lies the most genuine part
of the Reformers' view of the church.

At the Evangelical church meeting at Barmen, Germany, in 1934 it was necessary to take a stand on the
very pressing external situation caused by Hitler's
usurpation of power and the "German-Christian"
movement in the church. The Lutheran and the Reformed theologians assembled there adopted the
following definition of the church, based on Ephesians
4:15-16: "The Christian church is the community of
brothers where Jesus Christ in word and sacrament

through the Holy Spirit today acts as Lord. With its faith as well as its obedience, with its message as well as its order, in the midst of the world of sin and as the church of forgiven sinners, it shall witness that it is his property alone, that it only lives and will live in and by his solace and under his leadership in the expectation of his return."

The unique and gripping note in this is the Evangelical meeting's use of the same biblical passage for the basic concept of the church as Pope Pius XII did in his encyclical: "Christ as the head, the church as the body." However, a careful reading of the explanations of this expression reveals a significant difference. In the Evangelical explanation there is a border which may not be overstepped. The church is the body of Christ. Christ is truly in his church, completely and fully. But there can never be talk of any direct identification of Christ and the church. Christ is the free Lord, who in his unfathomable grace enters into his church and lives there, who in his word and work, as he chastises and resurrects, creates life out of the dead, erects his rule in the midst of a world of sin in spite of death and the devil. All this comes through the Holy Spirit in the word and the sacrament.

The church is not only an invisible "spiritual" fellowship, but a visible entity, as visible as that assembly of men which gathers about the word and the sacraments. "But a building, a preacher, a Bible, and an assemblage still does not create a church and a witness. All this will become a church and a witness only when God in his Spirit enters the scene," says a Reformed theologian.

"Let there be no doubt that where baptism and the gospel are, there are the saints," says Luther. For God's word is never ineffective. Where the gospel is truly heard, there the Spirit is at work, and there is a fellowship created which is the church. The church *is* not Christ, but wherever the living Christ speaks and works, there is his church. According to Luther, to believe in the church and the communion of saints means: "I believe that there is upon earth a holy assembly and congregation of pure Saints, under one head, even Christ, called together by the Holy Ghost in one faith, one mind and understanding, with manifold gifts, yet one in love. . . . I also am a part and member of the same, a participant and joint owner of all the good it possesses, brought to it and incorporated into it by the Holy Ghost . . ." (*The Large Catechism*).

The church has its signs. It has its voice, and it has its acts: baptism and Holy Communion. In these signs Christ is real and immanent in his church. "The Church is the congregation of saints in which the Gospel is rightly taught and the Sacraments rightly administered," says the Augsburg Confession. Where this happens, there by God's grace and power is the true church, because there is Christ himself with all his saving and creative power. In one of his writings Luther names as signs of the church the following: the word of God, baptism, the Eucharist, the power of the keys, i.e., confession and absolution, the office of preaching, prayer in which we publicly praise and thank God, the cross, and suffering.

The church can never become completely and absolutely static. It is always something that happens. It is that place upon this old world where the new world, the kingdom of God, is constantly breaking through the old world's *sacro egoismo*, where all human pride is broken. But it is also the place where mercy breaks through to the poor, the humble, and the despised and where sins are forgiven. Here true fellowship is created between men no matter how different they are. Here is atonement both between God and man and between men. And also between churches!

The church is the working place of the Holy Spirit on earth. It was born in the miracle of Pentecost and will live until Christ comes again to establish the kingdom in all its visible glory. It is the "place" and the "organ" of the kingdom of God here on earth. It does not stand as a fellowship of particularly dedicated or particularly religious men but a community of brothers, i.e., of ordinary men of the world who through the atonement and resurrection in Christ have been set free to live together in the genuine fellowship for which God has created man, but which sin has destroyed.

The church is not something separated and unique in this world; rather it is this world, with its created men, with its fields and forests, with its work and strain, with life in family and position, but also this world in its fall and sin—brought back by Christ to God. In the church the beginning of the new world takes place here and now. It is not itself the kingdom of God, but it exists for the sake of that kingdom. It has its constant limits in the kingdom of God but also its content and secret as well.

Through this the church is seen as an eschatalogical magnitude. It points beyond itself to that kingdom

that is yet to come. It appears in this world in hidden-
ness and ambiguity, always under "the sun of Satan,"
tempted to apostasy and emancipation and yet under
God's mighty promise. God himself will accomplish
his kingdom, that kingdom of which the church is the
beginning. This is the place of the church in the great
drama of the kingdom, as a link in God's plan of salvation. It is a realization of God's plan "according to his
purpose which he set forth in Christ as a plan for the
fulness of time, to unite all things in him, things in
heaven and things on earth" (Eph. 1:9-10).

The crucified and risen Christ, living and immanent
through the Holy Spirit in the word and sacrament,
freely and mercifully enters into his created and fallen
humanity and acts as Lord. In atoning and redeeming
and destroying the work of the devil, he creates the
new world with that "one new man." He does so even
here and now to the Ephesians—that one letter of the
New Testament which more than any other deals with
these things.

In this basic view much of Roman and Evangelical
theology can join in a common "yes." But the ways
separate the moment there is talk of how this is realized
in the church.

ROMAN CATHOLIC INSIGHTS:

A SCRIPTURAL CONCEPT
OF THE BODY OF CHRIST

BARNABAS AHERN, C. P.

The Church as the Body of Christ

In one way or another all the New Testament writers have preserved the unique element which Jesus himself emphasized in his teaching. Both early and late traditions of the first-century Christian community repeat his doctrine that the service of God necessarily involves an intimate bond with the Son of Man. Jesus must be confessed (Matt. 10:32), must be served in the neighbor (Matt. 10:40; 25.40; Mk. 9:40), must be followed Mk. 8:34; Matt. 16:24; Lk. 9:23), must be clung to as the source of light and strength (Lk. 10:22; Matt. 11:27-30), must be counted as needful to life as the vine stock to the branch (Jn. 15:1-10).

In the Pauline corpus this bond is described as the union between a body and its members. The apostle introduces this theme for the first time in I Cor., employs it again in his epistle to the Romans, and completes his explanation of it in the epistle to Colossians.

Either he or his disciple fits the keystone into the arch of his doctrinal development with the clean-cut formulae of the letter to the Ephesians.

Prolegomena

To measure accurately the meaning of this phrase it is necessary to keep in mind the large Pauline context which forms the background of this formulation. Ultimately Paul's thought is rooted in the dominant theological motifs of the Old Testament *Heilageschichte* which Christ brought to consummation in fulfilling the divinely inspired hopes of Israel.

FIRST MOTIF: STRONG SENSE OF COMMUNITY

At Sinai God created a *people* for his glory: "You shall be to me a kingdom of priests, a holy nation" (Ex. 19:6). Historically, many vicissitudes intervened to disrupt this unity of group existence. Ideally, however, unity remained the pattern of Israel's life. God's single rule over his people concretized itself in the institutions of kingship and priesthood. The flock was to follow the lead of its appointed shepherds. The preaching of the prophets, mentors charismatically endowed, did not and could not rupture this divinely prepared framework. While rebuking the shepherds these men of the spirit never tampered with the institutions which they knew were essential to Israel's life.

Law and cult were equally important guidelines bind-

ing the people to God and to one another in the unity of
social life and worship. All dreams of the future, all
expectancy of the perfect Israel to come, were rooted
in an awareness that God's people must ever live as the
Qahal Jahweh, the worshipping assembly of God.

Even after Jeremias and Ezechiel formulated the principle of individual responsibility (Jer. 31:27-34; Ezech.
18), the bond of community consciousness remained
unbroken. The fervid piety of the Psalmists, though
vibrantly personal, flows from their awareness of
membership in the "people of God." Their joyous con-
fidence and agonizing sorrow are inseparably bound
up with the fate of the nation.

For Paul the Church is the "Israel of God" (Gal. 6:16),
created anew with perfect life by the salvation deed of
Christ. Though the apostle prefers to describe the
single units of the Church and also its totality as the
ekklēsia rather than the *synagogē,* he still identifies it
as the Qahal bound to God by the family pact of the
"new covenant" sealed with the blood of Christ (cf.
II Cor. 3:14 with I Cor. 11:25). Under Paul's pen the
"vine" theme of the Old Testament (cf. Is. 5) becomes
the "olive tree" allegory of Rom. 11:17 ff.; but the
theme of unity remains the same. The members of the
"new Israel" bear the very names which were first
applied to the Israelites of old; they are "the saints,"
"the chosen." True to Paul's thought, the epistle to the
Ephesians introduces another Old-Testament covenant
term to describe the church. Like ancient Israel it is the
peripoiēsis, God's "special possession" (Eph. 1:14; cf.
Ex. 19:5).

SECOND MOTIF: CORPORATE PERSONALITY

The biblical principle of solidarity is fundamental to Paul's teaching. His doctrine on the role of Christ rests on the totality thought pattern of the Semite. The identification of the one with the many, of the father with his progeny, of the representative with the represented is characteristic both of the Old Testament and of Pauline concepts.

The eponymic features of the history of Abraham, Esau and Jacob, and of Jacob's twelve sons rests on the principle that the father incorporates his sons. As the root contains and determines the growth, indeed, the character of a tree, so do the patriarchs, particularly the first of them, give direction to the lives of their descendants. What transpired in the lives of men was read back into the story of the first man; that is why he is called *Adam*, mankind.

This same factor accounts for the fluidity of Israel's prophetic message. Now it is Israel the nation who will enter on the blessings of the messianic age; in the next breath it is a favored individual who alone features in the vision of the future. In the first three "servant Songs" of Isaiah, Israel the nation is Jahweh's Servant. In the last song, the fourth, an individual emerges who incorporates in himself the mission and destiny of his people. In Daniel it is the "saints of Israel" who pass through messianic tribulation. When, however, it comes time for reward the focus sharpens to a single individual—"one like unto a son of man"—who receives glory, honor, and dominion (Dan. 7:13-18). There is no contradiction here. In the mind of Israel's seers the individual embodies in himself, as a corporate personality, all those to whom he is inseparably joined. Whatever is realized in him is realized in and for them.

This Hebrew concept of "corporate personality," which Wheeler Robinson[1] and T. W. Manson[2] have shown to be essential for understanding Old Testament messianic prophecy, is essential also to Paul's concept of the role of Christ. Like Adam he, too, is a "corporate personality," a new Adam (I Cor. 15:22, 45-49; Rom. 5:14-19); through the law of solidarity his death and resurrection are efficacious for all: "We have come to the conclusion that, since one died for all, therefore all died" (II Cor. 5:14).

THIRD MOTIF: DEPENDENCE ON JAHWEH-JESUS

A third recurring theme in Paul is also rooted in the Old Testament. Israel of old was to trust in God and to depend completely upon him. Its whole life rested *beJahweh*—on Jahweh.

A transfer was inevitable in the life of the new Israel. Time and again Paul stresses the fact that the community and the individual are "in Christ." Deissmann's study of this phrase interpreted it in the locative sense,[3]

[1] H. Wheeler Robinson, "The Hebrew Conception of Corporate Personality," *Werden und Wesen des Alten Testaments* (*BZAW* 66, 1936), 46 ff.

[2] T. W. Manson, *The Servant-Messiah* (Cambridge: University Press, 1953), 74 with bibliography.

[3] Adolf Deissmann, *Die Neutestamentliche Formel "In Christo Jesu"* (Marburg, 1892) and *Paul* 2nd ed. (New York: Harper, 1927), chap. 6.

with the result that many thought of "Christ" as a mystical atmosphere in which the Christian lived. Recent research, however, has identified this phrase as the New Testament equivalent of the Old Testament *beJahweh.*[4] The church is established solidly on the foundation of Christ, drawing all its strength and stability from him. He who is the *Kyrios* gloriously reigning in heaven rules and empowers his people upon earth through the *pneuma* which is the messianic gift *par excellence.* This spirit of God and of Jesus is the active agent in the church's life; he it is who brings the saving power of Christ into the lives of men: "The *Kyrios* (in his active control of the church) is the *pneuma*" (II Cor. 3:17).

These three themes which recur in Paul's writings must be kept in mind if we are to understand fully his doctrine on the Church as the Body of Christ.

Paul's Reason for His Use of the Word "Body"

Many explanations have been given why the Apostle chose this expression. The most significant reason, however, is to be found in a statistical study of its occurrence. For the following survey we are indebted to E. Schweizer:[5]

[4] L. Cerfaux has made unceasing effort to correct the false notion that has issued from Deissmann's monograph. Cf. *Christ in the Theology of St. Paul,* tr. G. Webb-A. Walker (New York: Herder, 1959), 324-343; *The Church in the Theology of St. Paul,* tr. G. Webb-A. Walker (New York: Herder, 1959), 262-281; cf. also A. Wikenhauser, *Pauline Mysticism,* tr. J. Cunningham (New York: Herder and Herder, 1960), *passim.*

[5] E. Schweizer, "The Church as the Missionary Body of Christ," *New Testament Studies,* VIII (1961), 4-5.

Excluding the special usage of 'body' meaning 'corpse' or 'slave', we find that, even by counting the synoptic passages two or three times, out of 124 occurrences ninety-one are to be found in the Pauline letters (excluding the Pastorals). Focusing on the generally accepted letters, we meet the term sixty-nine times in the letters to the Corinthians and the Romans—the letter written in Corinth—and only four times elsewhere. This is illuminating. The term 'body' had been shaped in the discussion of the apostle with his opponents in Corinth. There Paul met a theological concept of man's divine 'spirit' being the only essential part of him. According to that, the physical body was to be taken off in death whereas the long-since deified spirit simply lived on, so that no further resurrection was needed (I Cor. 15:12). The physical body with its boundaries and limitations was also left behind when speaking in tongues which was considered the supreme gift of God (I Cor. 12:14). For the physical body 'all things were lawful' (I Cor. 6:12), since nothing mattered. Knowledge about this inner divine essence was the only essential thing, one's fellowmen were unimportant, even nuisances if they did not possess the same wisdom (I Cor. 8:1 ff.) The Lord's supper was a medicine for immortality; therefore it did not matter at all how one conducted the meal which preceded it (I Cor. 11:17 ff.). In opposition to such a concept, Paul presses the point that it is exactly in the body, that is, man in his earthly life, in the wholeness of his existence, that faith is to be lived.

Meaning of the Word "Body"

It is necessary to delay for a moment over Schweizer's phrase, "man . . . in the wholeness of his existence." This phrase is essential for an understanding of what Paul means by "body."

As a Hebrew writing on religious themes, he speaks of

the body not as a neutral element in the body-soul composite of Greek anthropology but rather as the whole animated body-person whose thoughts and desires are contained and manifested under the sensible aspect of somatic experience. Though it is an exaggeration to say that the Hebrew mentality knew nothing of the body in a restricted and neutral sense, it is quite correct to say that a Hebrew using the word "body" in a religious context includes in that term the whole person.[6]

When, therefore, Paul describes the union of the individual Christian with Christ as the union of "body" with "body" he introduces an element of intimacy and realism which cannot be forgotten in explaining his classic description of the Church as the "body of Christ." To explain this phrase as a mere borrowing from the vocabulary and thought patterns of the Stoa is to overlook the realism of Paul's earliest teaching on the bond between Christ and the Christian.

The Body Theme in I Cor. 6:14-17

Paul's first allusion to the "Body-of-Christ" theme introduces it not so much as a master principle of his system but as the emergent of a particular context. He writes of it because he chooses to challenge an ugly problem on the level of its own realism.

Christians of Corinth had fallen back into fornication,

[6] J. A. T. Robinson, *The Body: A Study in Pauline Theology* (Chicago: Regnery, 1952), pp. 26-28 and *passim*. This book should be read with the reservations noted by P. Benoit in his review of it in *RB*, LXIV (1957), 581-583.

into the commingling of body with body not merely as a physical experience but as a full personal and psychic interchange of thought and affection. Paul opposes the sin by appealing to another bond which the Christian has already contracted, the well-known bond between his *sōma* and the *sōma* of the glorified Christ, which is as real as the union between a man and a harlot: "Do you not know that your bodies are members of Christ? Shall I then take the members of Christ and make them members of a harlot" (I Cor. 6:15)? In both cases the full person is involved. *Sōma* is not merely the physical element in the body-soul composite; for Paul the Hebrew it is the whole self as an animated body vital with the fullness of personality.

It is true, the union between a man and a harlot has in it only the weakness and earthiness of *sarx*: "He who cleaves to a harlot becomes one body with her. 'For the two,' it says, 'shall be in one flesh'." On the other hand, the union between the Christian and the glorified Christ is vital with the strength and holiness of *pneuma*: "He who cleaves to the Lord is one spirit with him" (I Cor. 6:17). Nevertheless, whether the union be in "flesh" or in "spirit" (in the Pauline sense of apart from God or in God), it is always the full body-person that is involved.[7]

[7] P. Benoit, "Corps, Tete et Plérôme," *RB*, LXIII (1956), 13, n. 5: "C'est par opposition au soma uni à la courtisane sous son aspect de *sarx* que Paul ecrit ici *pneuma*, il songe en réalité au sōma pneumatikon du Christ ressuscite, dont le chretien est un membre." Cf. E. Percy, *Der Leib Christ in den paulinischen Homoloquomena und Antilegomena* (Lund: Glearup-Harrassowitz, 1942), pp. 14 f.

The Body Theme in Rom. 7:4

Again in Rom. 7:14 it is obviously the course of context which leads Paul to speak of Christians belonging to the risen body of the Saviour in language which is uncompromisingly physical. In treating of the Christian's relation to the law and to Christ he has introduced the example of a woman free to marry another after the death of her husband. On the basis of this example he goes on to describe the Christian's new relation to Christ as physically real and personal as that of man and wife: "We have been made to die to the law, so as to belong to another who has risen from the dead, in order that we may bring forth fruit unto God" (Rom. 7:4).

These first allusions to the body of Christ are thus incidental, the emergent of a given context. Yet they have a validity all their own because they aptly express the realism of the Christian's union with Christ as Paul sees it and as he, or his disciple, will express it later in the consummate synthesis of his thought (Eph. 5:25-32) where he likens the union of Christ and his church to the bond between a devoted husband and his wife. No union could be more intimate, because no dependence could be more complete. All that the Christian has as a Christian he receives in the total surrender of his body-person to the body-person of Christ: "You are in Christ Jesus, who has become for us God-given wisdom, and justice, and sanctification, and redemption" (I Cor. 1:30-31).[8]

[8] This text probably expresses better than any other the Christian's subjective participation in the mediation of Christ. W. L.

Incorporation Through Baptism

This union begins at baptism, as Paul indicates in Gal.
3:27-28. Though shifting his thought pattern he maintains the dynamic realism of the Christian experience:
"All you who have been baptized into Christ have put
on Christ." The analogy is drawn from the action of
putting on a garment; but, as G. Duncan[9] points out,
"In Scripture it denotes that the wearer becomes in a
subtle way identified with what he puts on." Thus God
is clothed with majesty (Ps. 92:1); the arm of the Lord
puts on strength (Is. 51:9); the wicked are clothed with
shame and disgrace (Ps. 34:26); Job puts on justice
(Jb. 29:14). The same use of *endyesthai* is found also,
though rarely, in classical Greek where it signifies
similarly entering into another's dispositions.[10] Paul
employs this figure fifteen times. The present text
shows how intimate is the identification which it
evokes.[11] For he goes on to affirm that in the psycho-
somatic rite of baptism the body-person of the Christian is so totally surrendered to Christ that whatever is

Knox, *St. Paul and the Church of the Gentiles* (Cambridge:
University Press, 1939), p. 11t. n. 1, has called attention to its
importance.

[9] G. Duncan, *The Epistle of St. Paul to the Galatians* (Moffatt
NTC) (London: Hodder and Stoughton, 1934), p. 123.

[10] Dionysius Halicarn., *Antiquitates Romanae*, 11,5: *ton Tar-
kynion endyesthai*; Libanius, *Epistulas*, 1048, 2: *ripsas stratioten
enedy ton sophistēn.* Cf. A. Oepke, *ThWNT* 2, 319-20.

[11] St. John Chrysostom, commenting on Gal. 3:28 (*PG* 61:656),
observes that St. Paul has exhausted every means of expressing
the intimacy of this union until finally he describes the Christian as manifesting Christ in himself (*en autō deiknys ton
Christon*).

merely *sarx* disappears, so that "There is neither slave nor freeman; there is neither male nor female. For you are all one (*'eis*—masculine) in Christ Jesus" (Gal. 3:28).

Paul therefore teaches clearly that Christian life involves a real and personal union between the individual *sōma* of the Christian and the individual *sōma* of the glorified Christ, a union so intimate that the body-person of the Saviour alone functions as the directive spiritual force. If they are two in one spirit, there is no doubt to whom the spirit belongs: "I live, now not I, but Christ lives in me" (Gal. 2:20).

Body Union through the Eucharist

This same realism prevails when Paul comes to speak of Christians as a collectivity in his discussion of the Eucharist. Once more the point of departure for his memorable statement is a particular problem, the danger of syncretism arising from sharing in the banquets of pagan worship. He declares that such conduct is incompatible with the celebration of the Christian supper which joins the Christian to Christ: "The bread that we break, is it not the sharing (*koinōnia*) of the body of the Lord" (I Cor. 10:16)?

As proof of this real presence of Christ in the Eucharist Paul appeals to a fact which carried a barbed thrust to the disunited Corinthians. He recalls the truth which was recognized from the beginning (cf. Acts 2:42): the remarkable *koinōnia* of Christian fellowship—the unity of many with one another—has its total cause in the *koinōnia* of each individual with Christ in the breaking of the bread: "Because the bread is one, we though many, are one body, we who partake of the one bread" (I Cor. 10:17).[12] In this text the "one body" is still the individual body-person of the risen Christ. There is nothing here to urge that Paul is beginning to use the Stoic analogue as a metaphor for the social organization of the church.[13] The "many" are "one body" because communion makes each one concorporeal with Christ. In the realism of Paul's thought, both baptism and communion enable the risen Saviour to become "all in all" (cf. I Cor. 12:13). Indeed, Dr. Rawlinson[14] is on firm ground when he emphasizes the importance of the Eucharist as a prime element in shaping Paul's doctrine on the church as the body of Christ.

Body Theme in I Cor. 12 and Rom. 12

Here one is more tempted to find a metaphorical sense in Paul's extended discussion of the body of Christ. Familiar as he was with the expressions and thought patterns of the Stoa,[15] he could have used their classic body theme as a metaphor to describe the unity in

[12] S. Lyonnet, "La 'Koinōnia' de l'Église primitive et la sainte Eucharistie," *Actas del XXXV Congreso Eucaristico Internacional Barcelona*, 1952, Sesiones de Estudio 1, pp. 5111-5115; M. Fraeyman, "Fractio panis in communitate primitiva," *Collationes Brugenses et Gandavenses* (1955), pp. 370-373.

[13] L. Cerfaux, *The Church in the Theology of St. Paul*, 278-279.

[14] Dr. Rawlinson, "Corpus Christi," *Mysterium Christi*, ed. G. K. Bell and A. Deissmann (Berlin, 1931), pp. 275-296.

[15] A Fridrichsen, "Zum Thema 'Paulus und die Stoa'," *Coniect. neotestam.*, IX (1944), 27-31; J. Nelis, "Les antithèses litteraires dans les Épîtres de saint Paul," NRT, LXX (1948), 360-387.

diversity which characterized the church as a social body with its distinct functions and members.[16]

Paul's concept, however, is rooted in a fact which the Stoic never dreamed of. If he describes the church as the body of Christ it is primarily because he sees each Christian as *syssōmos* with Christ through the transforming influence of Christ's spirit: "Indeed we were all brought into one body by baptism, in the one spirit" (I Cor. 12:13). At baptism Christ shares with the man of faith the spirit who inspired and ruled his own human life. The spirit of Jesus becomes the spirit of his follower. This is the whole burden of Paul's thought in Rom. 8—a chapter which he has anticipated succinctly in a single sentence: "To prove that you are sons, God has sent into our hearts the spirit of his Son, crying 'Abba! Father!' " (Gal. 4:6).

Baptized into his body-person, Christians are constantly preserved in union with him by drinking of one spirit in the Eucharist (I Cor. 12:13).[17] This fact, far

---

[16] The Stoa instructed the true man to regard himself as a member of the body-universe; cf. Seneca, *Ep.* 92, 30; Epictetus, *Dissert.* 2,5,24; 2,5,26; 2,10,31. A number of pertinent texts from the Stoa are presented by A. Wikenhauser, *Die Kirche als der Mystische Leib nach dem Apostel Paulus* (Munster in West.: Aschendorff, 1937), pp. 130-143; cf. J. Dupont, *Gnosis, La connaissance religieuse dans les épîtres de saint Paul* (Louvain: Nauwelaerts, 1949), pp. 435-438.

[17] E. Percy, *Der Leib Christi*, p. 17, and R. Schnackenburg, *Das Heilsgeschehen bei der Taufe nach dem Apostel Paulus*, pp. 78-80, I, interpret the whole passage (v. 13) as referring to baptism, so that both members form a synonymous parallelism. However, in view of a previous reference to baptism as distinct from nourishment: food-drink (I Cor. 10:2-4), it seems more likely that the "drinking of the Spirit" is a reference to the Christian sacrament of nourishment, the Eucharist. This is the

more than a prevalent Greek terminology, prompted Paul to use the concept of body-unity in solving the bristling problem which had arisen at Corinth. If each Christian has his own role to play and his own gift to use, this is only to be expected, for the body of Christ, like any real body, must be differentiated into many members, all ruled and vivified by the same spirit.

The question immediately arises, "Is Paul then speaking of the risen body of the personal Christ, or is he speaking of a body apart from Christ yet vivified by him? *Tertium non datur.*" But even today this type of question is fair and valid only when both the questioner and the one giving answer are thinking in the same thought patterns. It would not be right to press Paul with this query for the simple reason that his thought here rises eminently above our thought and includes formalities which our thought patterns tend to differentiate. He knows and he has said clearly that every Christian is united really and corporally to the risen body of Christ. Concentrating on this thought of the allness and uniqueness of Christ, he has nothing left to say except that all Christians together must be the body of Christ. How this is possible is not his concern at this point. Canon Cerfaux[18] is content to translate Paul's words with the non-commital, "You are a body, a body which is that of Christ." It will be the later controversy with the Colossians which will render his expression precise in describing the nature of the

---

conclusion of E. Kasemann, *Leib und Leib Christi (Beitrage zur historischen Theologie)* (Tubingen, 1933), p. 176; P. Benoit, "Corps, Tete et Plérôme," *RB*, LXIII (1956), 15.

[18] *The Church in the Theology of St. Paul*, 277.

bond as the relation of head and members.[19] At the stage of I Cor., his thought is moving at a level of eminence and realism which is all-inclusive.

The Body Theme in Romans

In this epistle Paul simply presumes that his readers are familiar with the truth that Christian life has united them—body-person to body-person—with Christ. In developing his thought he is much more concerned to show the dynamic involvements of this union. In becoming a member of Christ's body one lives by his life and shares in all the salvific activity of him who died and rose again as the corporate person *par excellence*. In the first part of this epistle Christ, like another Adam, is seen at work in his task of dying and rising for men. In the second part the Christian shares dynamically in all that Christ is and has. So intimately is the baptized united to the body-person of the Saviour that his whole spiritual life becomes the death-life of Christ (Rom. 6:3-11) through the activity of the spirit who vivifies and glorifies the whole body-person of the Christian (Rom. 8).[20] In a word life *in Christ* is inseparably connected with and provides foundation for life *with Christ*.

This conclusion emerges clearly from the inadequacy of P. Bonnard's recent effort to present a definitive

[19] P. Benoit, "Corps, Tete et Plérôme," 18 ff.
[20] Cf. A. Feuillet, "Le Mystère Paschale et la Résurrection des chrétiens d'après les Épîtres pauliniennes," *NRT*, LXXIX (1957), 343. "Dans l'Épître aux Romains, il est certain que les deux tableaux des chapitres VI (délivrance par le Christ dans le baptême) et VIII (délivrance par l'Ésprit Saint) se correspondent et se complètent."

explanation of Paul's *syn*-phrases on the score of merely forensic justification.[21] After reviewing and pointing out the weaknesses of various explanations of this Pauline expression, "with Christ" (pp. 105-110), he makes his own suggestion that Paul has borrowed the use of *syn* from the Hellenistic liturgies, even though Bonnard must admit that there is nothing so far discovered in the literature of the mysteries to substantiate his claim (p. 110). As for the reality contained in the *syn*-phrase it consists totally in the mere assent of the individual, living in the present, to the unique and definitive fact of Christ's death and resurrection (pp. 111-112).

This proposal, however, carries the sign of its own weakness. The very fact that Bonnard traces the Pauline *syn*-phrase to the mystery literature (though confessedly without actual verification) shows his awareness that in the Pauline corpus this phrase is essentially dependent upon the believer's real and present share in the life of the Saviour, an element which is common to the teaching of Paul and the liturgy of the mystery cults.

Moreover, unless Paul's teaching on life *with Christ* is founded upon the realism of life *in Christ*, then Christian experience, as described in the Pauline epistles, is merely the human psychological effort of Jewish striving for justice. Indeed, the salvific event of Calvary is no more effective in the life of the individual than the divine intervention of Sinai unless the believer

[21] "Mourir et vivre avec Jésus-Christ selon saint Paul," *RHPhil Rel*, XXXVI (1956), 101-112. The page references in the text are all taken from this article.

shares by real participation in the action of the Saviour. In ruling out this real contact and in explaining Rom. 6:3-11 as descriptive of a mere mental attitude on the part of the believer, Bonnard is forced to reduce the baptismal liturgy to the commemorative value of the Pesach regulations in Ex. 13. This is precisely what he does (pp. 111-112; cf. p. 109).

The actual words of Paul, on the other hand (especially *symphytoi* in v. 5),[22] plus the whole background of Pauline doctrine in I Cor. make clear that he teaches a true and intimate union between the Christian and the risen Christ, in virtue of which the baptized actually shares all that Christ has accomplished as his representative. This truth is succinctly stated by S. Lyonnet:[23]

Strictly speaking, the Christ to whom St. Paul declares us united is always the glorious Christ; but, since he is a Christ who died and rose again, we, by the very fact of our union with him, share in the effects of his death and resurrection. It is in this sense that we are plunged into his death, are crucified and rise with him.

Body Theme in Colossians

By the time he finished his great epistles Paul had completed his teaching on the intimacy and realism of the Christian's union with the body of Christ. His doctrine, however, still needed more precise formulation. The

[22] P. Gächter, "Zur Exegese von Rom. 6:5," *ZKT*, LIV (1930), 88-92. All will not accept the author's conclusion that this verse involves an anacoluthon. However, his review of all proposed interpretations focuses attention on the general agreement that *symphytoi* involves the concept of real union.

[23] Note on Rom. 6:4 in J. Huby-S. Lyonnet, *Saint Paul, Épître aux Romains* (*VS* 10; Paris: Beauchesne, 1957), p. 590.

proven unity of the body of Christ had to be harmo-
nized with the obvious contrast which separates the
church on earth from the glorious *Kyrios* in heaven.

Paul found occasion to make this precise formulation
in his epistle to the Colossians. Christians at Colossae
had sought to place Christ in the framework of the
Hellenistic *plerōma* which had been created without
reference to him. In this they failed through undue
exaltation of intermediary beings (cf. Col. 2:17-18).

The apostle goes right to the heart of the crisis by
assigning Christ a pre-eminent role in the hierarchy of
celestial beings. He affirms the absolute supremacy of
Christ and presents him as head of all creation, its very
source and end (Col. 1:15-17). This cosmic exaltation
of the heavenly Christ influences Paul's expression of
his relation to the church. There, too, Christ is head
and the church is his body guided and vivified by his
spirit (Col. 1:18; 2:19).

In this new presentation Paul sacrifices nothing of his
earlier teaching on the realism of the bond uniting
Christ and the Christian. The church is still his body,
for he as head, in the Greek sense of *kephalē*, is the
sole source of its life (Col. 2:19; 3:3-4). Union with
him brings a full share in the salvific mystery of his
death-resurrection. (Paul's teaching on this theme in
Col. 2:11-13 parallels his earlier doctrine in Rom. 6:3-
11.) All Christian life, therefore, is life in and with
Christ (Col. 2:6-7; 3:1-4).

These themes of Colossians are resumed in the
masterly synthesis of Ephesians where Paul or his
disciple likens the union between Christ and the
Church to the physical-psychical union of husband and

wife (5:29-32) and at the same time incorporates the precise formulation of Colossians: "He put everything in subjection beneath his feet, and appointed him as supreme head to the church, which is his body and as such holds within it the fullness of him who himself receives the entire fullness of God" (Eph. 1:22-23).

The Body, the Kingdom, the New Israel

The body-of-Christ theme in Paul is intimately connected with the other focal points of doctrine which we have indicated in the prolegomena. The Christian united to the body of Christ lives with the complete dependence on him which marked Israel's relations to Jahweh. It is obvious, too, that Christ is able to enrich his body precisely because the saving deed of his death-resurrection was the act of a corporate person who embodied in himself all those with whom he would share his triumph and on whom he would pour forth his spirit.

It is just as important to note that all this takes place in the earthly ambient of the new Israel as Paul saw it in actual existence around him. Like Israel of the old covenant the new Israel is bound into unity by its distinctive teaching, by the authority of its appointed shepherds, and by cult and sacraments which feature appropriately in the psycho-somatic union between the body-person of Christ and the body-person of the believer.

If, therefore, Paul is the teacher of intimate union between Christ and the Christian, if he describes better than anyone else the transforming action of Christ's saving mysteries, if he is the theologian of the spirit which vivifies and guides the body of Christ, he is by that very fact an eminent ecclesiologist. For whatever he writes about the body of Christ centers in that human reality all around him, the church with its *kerygma* and *didache*, with its *episcopoi* and *presbyteroi*, with its baptism and "breaking of bread." That real Church *is* the body of Christ.

ROMAN CATHOLIC INSIGHTS:

A PATRISTIC UNDERSTANDING
OF THE BODY OF CHRIST

WALTER J. BURGHARDT, S. J.

The Body of Christ: Patristic Insights

A single paper on the Body of Christ in early Christian theology is a perilous project. The material is too
vast for analysis, too involved for synthesis. For the
purposes of the Notre Dame Colloquium, the desirable
approach was to suggest several overarching ideas—
ideas that are significant in themselves and reveal
scriptural roots, ideas stimulative of further development and provocative of spirited conversation in an
ecumenical milieu. In this context, the ideas can only
be outlined, not evolved; can only be illustrated, not
demonstrated. Most of the ancient Fathers never appear in person, and a generation of modern scholar-
ship is utilized with bare acknowledgment. Vast areas
of the patristic era are not explicitly mined; many pertinent facets of early Christian doctrine are merely
grazed; other theological ideas and insights would
complement, supplement, even at times challenge the

structure I rear. And when the reader's eye meets "the Fathers," he must be gracious enough to understand by that term "an impressive patristic tradition."

Patristic theology on the Body of Christ finds its springboard in St. Paul. It is Paul's doctrine that the Fathers develop, and this development takes a three-fold direction.[1]

First, St. Paul gives patristic theology the framework for the idea of the ontological inclusion of all men in Christ, the Second Adam. For the Fathers, the Incarnation as *assumptio hominis* has a collective as well as an individual aspect: it touches the one humanity of all men; it creates a real bond in Christ between the whole creature "man" and Christ.

Second, the oneness between humanity and Christ that was radically established in the Incarnation and progressively realized through the Cross, the Resurrection, and the Ascension, finds a unique consummation in the Eucharist, building on baptism. As the Fathers see it, you cannot understand the Eucharist without reference to the common *concorporatio cum Christo*; conversely, you cannot understand the Body of Christ without reference to the *sacramentum corporis Christi* as the source of the very being of Christ's Body. The Church is the Body of Christ because she lives by the body of Christ.

Third, this same Eucharist is the realization of fraternal love; for it represents fraternal love and demands it imperiously in the common participation of

[1] Cf. J. Ratzinger, "Leib Christi: II, Dogmatisch," *Lexikon für Theologie und Kirche* 6 (2nd ed.; Freiburg, 1961), 910.

all believers, without exception or discrimination, in one table. The sacramental includes the ethical.

Such, on broad lines, is the patristic evolution of St. Paul. Three realities, three mysteries, reveal the Body of Christ with incomparable clarity: Incarnation, Eucharist, and love. These are the three ideas I shall develop, with broad strokes, in this paper.

I INCARNATION

Patristic thought on the Incarnation and the Mystical Body is a complex thing. It reveals several facets, several stages, several moments, which should indeed be distinguished, but may never be isolated.

There is, to begin with, the first moment of the Incarnation, the moment of Mary's whispered yes, the unique moment when divinity and humanity were wed in the womb of a virgin. At that instant, some of the Fathers insisted, a basic, radical, fundamental kinship with God was realized by all humanity. The thesis was trumpeted in the West by Hilary of Poitiers: "Every man was in Christ Jesus."[2] "He has taken the body of each of us."[3] In virtue of the one body he took, all

[2] Hilary of Poitiers, *Comm. in Matt.* 2, 5 (*PL* 9: 927). In fact, the Latin is even more expressive: "Erat in Christo Iesu homo totus. . . ." Cf. also Hilary's *De trinitate* 2, 24 (*PL* 10: 66): ". . . ut . . . sanctificatum in eo universi generis humani corpus exsisteret. . . ." Also *ibid.* 2, 25 (*PL* 10: 67): ". . . nos eguimus ut Deus caro fieret, et habitaret in nobis, id est, assumptione carnis unius interna universae carnis incoleret."

[3] Hilary of Poitiers, *Comm. in Matt.* 19, 5 (*PL* 9: 1025). Once again the Latin is very expressive: "omnium nostrum corpus assumpsit. . . ."

humanity is contained in him.[4] But it was the East, the
Greek Fathers, that found here a theme of predilection.
And on this theme Cyril of Alexandria was remarkably
eloquent: "[Christ] has us in Himself, inasmuch as He
bore our nature, and the Word's body was called our
body."[5] He dwelt in all "through one."[6]

What do such affirmations mean? What is this radical
oneness of all men with Christ by the sheer fact of the
Incarnation? Here patrologists are not at peace. Is this
no more than Aristotle in Christian vesture? There is
but one species "man"; we are men; Christ was man;
therefore, we are one with Christ? Or is this Plato
badly disguised? A universal human nature "out
there"? A collective incarnation?

Patrologists are not at peace. There is, I suggest, a
basic affirmation that breaks through with relative
ease, and a more intimate exegesis that is not at all
easy. The basic affirmation is clear enough. A new oneness, a root unity, between man and God was conceived in Nazareth and brought to birth in Bethlehem.
For men like Athanasius, "the world is so truly one
whole that when the Word enters into it and becomes
one of our race, all things take on a new dignity."[7]
And here the point of contact, the meeting ground,
between God and man is the flesh of Christ, his humanity. At this stage, humanity is not yet the Body

[4] Cf. *ibid.* 4, 12 (*PL* 9: 935): ". . . in eo, per naturam suscepti
corporis, quaedam universi generis humani congregatio con-
tinetur."

[5] Cyril of Alexandria, *Comm. in Ioan.* 9, 1 (Pusey 2, 486).

[6] *Ibid.* 1, 9 (Pusey 1, 141).

[7] So E. Mersch, *The Whole Christ: The Historical Development
of the Doctrine of the Mystical Body in Scripture and Tradition*,
tr. J. R. Kelly (London, 1949), p. 273.

of Christ, alive with his life, thrilling to his divine touch. But humanity is ready, is poised on the edge of divinity. No longer is flesh simply the tinderbox of sin. If it has not yet begun to live with the life of Christ, it all but quivers with his breath. For the flesh that God took is our flesh; in some genuine sense, it is my flesh, your flesh, the flesh of every human being born into this world.

The more intimate exegesis is not easy. How do the early Christian writers explain this new link between God and man, between the Word and the world, between Christ and humanity in the Incarnation? Some make no effort to explain it; some are vexingly vague. Still, from the vast reaches of patristic literature Sebastian Tromp sees eight ideas emerge, eight reasons, eight facets of this all-inclusive incorporation of humanity into Christ.[8] (1) A common nature links us, consanguinity makes us one. (2) Every perfection of every man is a perfection Christ possesses to a more excellent degree. (3) Christ is the New Adam of the whole race, and so he can represent the race before God, play the mediator between God and man. (4) He contains all men in himself in the sense that he is archetype of the total humanity which he is to refashion in his own image. (5) To his glory all creatures are oriented, so that through him and with him and in him all honor and glory may be given to the Father through the Spirit. (6) All the supernatural life of all men is hidden in Christ as in its source. (7) All men are one with Christ in his loving knowledge: enfleshed

[8] Cf. S. Tromp, *Corpus Christi quod est ecclesia* 1: *Introductio generalis* (2nd ed.; Rome, 1946), pp. 30-31.

to save all men, he has all men present to him with all their actions, embraces them all with salvific love. (8) There is some Platonic speculation: just as nothing good or true can exist in the natural order unless it participates in the subsistent idea of the Good and the True, so in the heavenly order no one can live a genuinely heavenly life in truth and goodness unless he participates in the heavenly man, who is truth and life, who for us has been made wisdom and justice.

For all these reasons, or for any of them, patristic mentality found in the Incarnation itself the church in its conception. In the pregnant expression of Leo the Great, "the birth of the Head is the birth of the Body."[9]

So much for the first stage: a radical oneness between God and man effected at the Incarnation in the flesh of Christ. But this oneness, like the Incarnation itself, is but a beginning, a foundation, a pledge of the reality to come. And this reality comes on Calvary. If Christ's birth is the first stage, his death is the second. If the seed of the Mystical Body is planted in Bethlehem, it comes to life, to flower, on Calvary. Let me spell out this incandescent idea in a series of patristic propositions.

First, the Fathers insist that on the Cross Christ gave birth to the church, built it, fashioned and founded it, consecrated it. Clement of Alexandria is eloquent: "The Lord gave birth to [the Church] in the distress of

[9] Leo the Great, *Serm.* 26, 2 (*PL* 54: 213): "Generatio enim Christi origo est populi christiani, et natalis capitis natalis est corporis."

His flesh, wrapped her in the swaddling clothes of His precious blood."[10]

Second, with a special stress a number of Fathers affirm that the church of Christ was born from the side of Christ. That is why they see in the fashioning of Eve from the flesh of Adam a mystery of the church's origin. The church, as the New Eve, came forth from, was built out of, the side of the New Adam, as he slept the sleep of death on the Cross. This is a favorite theme of the Fathers, played at times with subtle variations; I shall illustrate it from Chrysostom in the East and Augustine in the West. Chrysostom is splendidly expressive:

For just as Eve was produced from the side (*pleuras*) of Adam, so too we from the side of Christ. This, you see, is the meaning of the phrase 'from his flesh and from his bones' (Gen. 2:21). That Eve was produced from the side of Adam, this we all know; and Scripture has told us in clear terms that [God] cast a trance upon Adam, took one of his ribs (*pleurōn*), and built up the woman. But that the church took shape from the side of Christ, where could we find proof of this? This too Scripture reveals. For after Christ was lifted up on the Cross, was nailed thereto, and

[10] Clement of Alexandria, *Paedagogus* 1, 6, 42 (*GCS* 12, 115). I have translated the Greek verb *ekuēsen* "gave birth to" rather than "conceived," in the light of the clause that closes the sentence. For the context, the lacunae in the text, and an exegesis, cf. J. C. Plumpe, *Mater Ecclesia: An Inquiry into the Concept of the Church as Mother in Early Christianity* (Washington, D.C., 1943), pp. 64-67. I do not think Clement and Leo (cf. supra n. 9) are really at odds on the birth of the church; for the metaphor of birth can, and in patristic ecclesiology does, involve several stages.

died, 'one of the soldiers came nigh and pierced His side, and there came forth blood and water' (Jn. 19:34). From that blood and water the whole Church has its being and existence (*synestēke*). To this Christ Himself bears witness when He says: 'Unless one be born again of water and spirit, he cannot enter the kingdom of heaven' (Jn. 3:5). Blood He calls spirit. In point of fact, we are born through the water of baptism and we are nourished by [His] blood. Do you see how we are from His flesh and from His bones, we who have our birth and our nourishment from His blood and from water? Just as the woman was fashioned from Adam in sleep, so the Church was formed from the side of Christ in death.[11]

Augustine thinks and writes in the same tradition:

This is the reason why the first woman was made from the side (*latere*) of the man while he slept, and was called life and mother of the living. A great good did she betoken, before the great evil of her transgression. Here the Second Adam with bowed head slept upon the Cross, that therefrom a wife might be formed for Him—that which flowed forth from His side (*latere*) as He slept. O death from which the dead come to life again![12]

11 John Chrysostom, *Laus Maximi et Quales ducendae sint uxores* 3 (*PG* 51: 229).
12 Augustine, *Tract. in Ioan.* 120, 2 (*CCL* 36, 661). For an earlier example of this typology, see Methodius, *Symposium* 3, 8 (*GCS* 27, 35-36; tr. H. A. Musurillo, *ACW* 27, 65-66). Methodius explicitly refers the story of Adam and Eve to Christ and the church: this is Paul's "mystery" (Eph. 5:32). He insists that Paul "could apply directly to Christ, as arrows to their mark, all that was said of Adam. Thus would it be in excellent accord with this that the Church has been formed from His flesh and bone. For it was for her sake that the Word left His heavenly Father and came down to earth in order to cling to His Spouse, and slept in the ecstasy of His Passion. . . . And it is impossible for anyone to participate in the Holy Spirit and to be counted

Third, as Augustine has just indicated, on the Cross
the church was wed to Christ. The church is to Christ
what Eve was to Adam: she is his spouse, his bride.
In the striking sentence of a sermon to catechumens
falsely attributed to Augustine: "De sponso sponsa
nascitur, et ut nascitur statim illi coniungitur; at tunc
sponsa nubit, quando sponsus moritur; et tunc ille
sponsae coniungitur, quando a mortalibus separa-
tur."[13]

Fourth, on the Cross the church received from Christ
a new life, the gifts of the Holy Spirit—in fact, the
Spirit himself. Caesarius of Arles and Gregory the
Great reach back into the Old Testament, recall Elisha
bending down and breathing seven times on the life-
less boy, and tell us that Elisha prefigures Christ on the
Cross, giving life to the church through the seven gifts
of the Spirit. For the external structure of the church
clothes an inner life that is Christ's life, pulsing
through the members of the Body like another blood-
stream. The Spirit that quickens this Body is the Holy
Spirit, who links human beings with one another and
with Christ. This is early Christian thinking, as you
find it, for example, in Gregory the Great:

a member of Christ unless again the word has first descended
upon him and fallen into the sleep of ecstasy, that he may rise
from his own deep sleep and, filled with the Spirit, receive a
renewal and rejuvenation. Now the side (*pleura*) of the Word
may truly be called the Spirit of Truth which is septiform according to the prophet; and God, taking from Christ's side
during His ecstasy, that is, after His Incarnation and Passion,
prepares for Him a helpmate, that is to say, all souls who are
betrothed and wedded to Him. . . ."

[13] Ps.-Augustine, *De symbolo: Sermo 1 ad catechumenos* 6, 15
(*PL* 40: 645).

. . . Christ with His whole Church . . . is one person. And as the soul is one (soul) which gives life to the various members of the body, so the one Holy Spirit quickens and illuminates the whole Church. For as Christ, who is the Head of the Church, was conceived of the Holy Spirit, so the holy Church, which is His Body, is filled by the same Holy Spirit that it may have life, is fortified by His power that it may subsist in the structure of one faith and one love.[14]

Once again Augustine sums up patristic mentality in a pithy sentence: "What the soul is to the body of a man, this the Holy Spirit is to the Body of Christ, which is the Church: what the soul does in all the members of one body, this the Holy Spirit does in the whole Church."[15]

Fifth, because the church comes forth from the side of Christ as the New Eve fecundated by the Spirit of Christ, the church that comes into being on the Cross is a mother: mother of the faithful, mother of the living. As early as the year 210, Tertullian argued that if Adam prefigured Christ, then the sleep of Adam typified the death of Christ. During the sleep of Adam, the first mother, Eve, was fashioned from his side. So then, in God's plan Christ was to submit to the sleep

[14] Gregory the Great, *In septem ps. poenit. exp.*: Ps. 101 (*PL* 79: 602).

[15] Augustine, *Serm.* 267, 4 (*PL* 38: 1231). For firsthand information on the patristic understanding of the Holy Spirit as Soul of the Mystical Body, see the two volumes in which S. Tromp has gathered the principal texts of the Greek and Latin Fathers respectively: *De Spiritu sancto anima corporis mystici* 1: *Testimonia selecta e patribus graecis*; 2: *Testimonia selecta e patribus latinis* (Rome, 1932).

of death, that from the wound in his side "the true mother of the living, the Church, might be fashioned (*figuraretur*)."[16] "The implication," comments J. C. Plumpe, "is clear: as our physical life is from Adam through our first mother, Eve, so our entire spiritual life is derived ultimately from Christ, the Second Adam, through our Second Mother, the Church."[17]

In summary: it is on Calvary that the Body of Christ was born . . . born from the lanced side of the Crucified . . . at once spouse of Christ and mother of Christians . . . whose principle of life is the Spirit of Christ, that Holy Spirit whose function in the Body is to make Christians one with one another in Christ, by linking them through Christ in himself to the Father.

So much for the first two stages: the radical oneness between God and man effected at the Incarnation in the flesh of Christ, and the flowering of this seed on Calvary in the birth of the Mystical Body from the torn flesh of the crucified. A third stage is discoverable in the resurrection and ascension of Christ.

For the Fathers, the resurrection and ascension of Christ are not primarily theses in apologetics, proofs of divinity. It is not simply an individual that rises radiant from the dead and stands splendent before the Father; it is a nature. It is not merely the body born of

[16] Tertullian, *De anima* 43, 10 (Waszink, ed. 1947, p. 60). I incline to believe that here "figuraretur" has its proper meaning, "fashioned" (cf. "*de* iniuria lateris," as well as the reference to Eve), rather than a prefiguring, a representing, an allegorizing, a symbolizing, a signifying. Tertullian uses the word in both senses; cf. *Thesaurus linguae latinae, s.v.* "figuro."

[17] Plumpe, *Mater Ecclesia*, p. 57.

Mary in a manger that triumphs over death; it is the Body born of Christ on the wood. Listen to Gregory of Nyssa:

Since it was necessary that our whole nature be raised up from the dead, [God] stooped down to the corpse that we were, reached out His hand, so to speak, to man where he lay. He even drew so near to death as to grasp mortality and give to human nature the principle of the resurrection in His own body: by His power He raised up the whole of man with Himself [*or:* together]. The man who received God (*ho theodochos anthrōpos*), the man who through the resurrection was raised up with the divinity, came from no other source than our compound. Now just as in our body the activity of any one of the senses is jointly experienced in the whole organism linked to it, so, as if all human nature were a single human being *(henos tinos zōou)*, the resurrection of one of its members extends through the entire body, and because of the continuity and unity of our nature, it communicates itself from the part to the whole.[18]

Similarly, the ascension of Christ is the ascension of all humanity. Listen to Cyril of Alexandria as he discovers in this mystery an adoption of human nature, a sonship of all men with reference to the Father that is akin to the oneness achieved in the Incarnation:

Christ did not ascend to exhibit Himself to God the Father; for He was and is and always will be in the Father. . . . He

---

[18] Gregory of Nyssa, *Oratio catechetica magna* 32, 3-4 (Méridier, pp. 144-146; *PG* 45: 80 is seriously defective). As for "the man that received God," J. H. Srawley has pointed out succinctly in his translation, *The Catechetical Oration of St. Gregory of Nyssa* (London, 1917), p. 93, n. 2: "This language is inexact according to later theological standards. But Gregory is writing before Nestorianism had arisen."

ascended on this occasion as man, for a strange and unac-
customed manifestation, the Word who of old was without
humanity. For us and for our sakes He did this, in order
that, man that He was, He might hear addressed to Him in
His wholeness, as Son in power and with flesh, the words,
'Sit at my right hand' (Ps. 109:1), and transmit the glory
of sonship to the whole race through Himself. . . . He manifested Himself as man, in order to set us once more in the
sight of the Father, we who had gone from His gaze by
reason of the primeval transgression. He sat down as Son,
that we too might be called sons through Him and children
of God. . . .[19]

In patristic theology, the glorification of Christ is the
glorification of humanity; the glory of the Head is the
glory of the members. The language of Athanasius is
strong and uncompromising:

When Peter says, 'Let, therefore, the whole house of
Israel know with certainty that God has made Him both
Lord and Christ, this Jesus whom you crucified' (Acts 2:36),
it is not of His divinity that Peter says God made Him both
Lord and Christ; it is of His humanity, which is the whole
Church—the Church which is lord and king in Him after
His crucifixion, and is anointed for the kingdom of heaven,
that it may rule with Him who emptied Himself for it and
took it to Himself through the form of a slave.[20]

A summary of this initial patristic insight is in order.
For the Fathers, the Incarnation as *assumptio hominis*

[19] Cyril of Alexandria, *Comm. in Ioan.* 9 (Pusey 2, 404).
[20] Athanasius, *De incarn. et c. Arianos* 21 (*PG* 26: 1021). M.
Simonetti has denied the authenticity of this work, but, as J.
Quasten observes, "no convincing reasons have been advanced
against the Athanasian authorship" (*Patrology* 3 [Westminster,
Md., 1960], 28).

has a collective as well as an individual aspect: it touches the one humanity of all men and creates a real, ontological bond between the whole creature "man" and God. This Incarnation, however, is not an isolated event totally captured in the second chaptèr of St. Luke. It commences, it begins, with the conception of Christ and his birth; for this mystery creates a radical oneness between God and man in the flesh of Christ— radical because it is the requisite root, the indispensable foundation, of the properly supernatural oneness that will flower therefrom. The Incarnation reaches a high point, a peak, with the death of Christ on Calvary; for it is at this moment that the Body of Christ is truly born: at the instant that his physical body bows to death, his Mystical Body springs to life. And Calvary itself finds consummation in Christ's resurrection and ascension; for it is here that the Body of Christ—the Mystical Body in the physical body—stands before the Father resplendent with the life of Christ through the Spirit.

Note carefully, in this whole process, the role of the flesh, of Christ's humanity. This is the meeting ground between man and God. Hilary of Poitiers put it pithily: "The Word [who is] God became flesh, that through God-the-Word-made-flesh the flesh might progress unto (*proficeret in*) God the Word."[21] The process which the Greek Fathers called "divinization" is splendidly clear. Through the Incarnation humanity comes into contact with the humanity of Christ; through his humanity it comes into contact with his divinity;

---

[21] Hilary of Poitiers, *De trinitate* 1, 11 (*PL* 10: 33).

through his divinity it comes to share in the life of the Trinity.

II EUCHARIST

Now for the second patristic insight. The first focused on the origins of the Body of Christ in the life of Christ; the second focuses on the evolution of that Body in the life of the Christian. The first problem was: How did the Body of Christ come to be? The second problem is: How does one live the life of that Body? What gives the Body of Christ its unique unity? Where shall we discover its dynamism?

The patristic stress, I suggest, is on two liturgical rites: baptism and the Eucharist. For clarity's sake, let me present these two emphases in the form of orderly discourse. First, what is the role of baptism in the Body of Christ. The patristic response, on broad lines, is clear enough: it is through baptism that the individual is first incorporated into Christ. Understandably, the one same doctrine finds varied expression; it is shaded by the personality of the writer, suited to the need of the moment, tailored to the pressures of polemics. But through every nuance, across every new emphasis, the basic affirmation remains the same: it is by baptism that the Spirit makes men one in Christ Jesus.

Irenaeus, for example, insists that the church is the continuation of Christ; that, like Christ, the church has two facets, one visible, the other invisible; that her visible face is discoverable in the succession of bishops;

that in union with these episcopal sees divine life is communicated; that it is within the Body of Christ that the Holy Spirit continues the work he began in Christ. And he writes: ". . . just as it is impossible with dry wheat to form one mass or one loaf without water, even so we many could not become one in Christ Jesus without the water that is from heaven."[22]

Arguing against the Arian idea of a sheerly moral unity whether among the divine persons or among the faithful, Hilary of Poitiers asks:

The fact that amid so imposing a diversity of nationalities, of circumstances, and of sexes they [the faithful] are one—does this come about by an agreement of wills, or is it [not rather] effected by the unity of the mystery (*sacramenti*), because their baptism is one and all have put on one Christ? What has harmony of minds and wills to do here? They are one because they have been clothed with one Christ through the nature of one baptism.[23]

Chrysostom, entranced as so often by St. Paul, concludes that all the faithful are of the same family, and the family is Christ; all are one person, and the person is Christ; and this one family, this one person, is fashioned in baptism.

[22] Irenaeus, *Adv. haer.* 3, 18, 1 (Harvey 2, 92-93; in *PG* 7: 930 the book, chapter, and paragraph respectively are 3, 17, 2). It may be plausibly argued from the context that "the water that is from heaven" is the Holy Spirit. I suggest, however, that both the Spirit and the water of baptism are intended (cf. Jn. 3:5)—this on the basis of the sentence with which he tries to justify the thesis we have quoted: "Corpora enim nostra *per lavacrum* illam, quae est ad incorruptionem, unitatem acceperunt, animae autem *per Spiritum*" (*ibid.*; Harvey 2, 93).
[23] Hilary of Poitiers, *De trinitate* 8, 8 (*PL* 10: 242).

Why did [Paul] not say, 'All of you who were baptized into Christ have been born of God'? For this is what we would expect, if he is to show that they are sons. But Paul puts this truth in a manner more awesome. For if Christ is the Son of God, and if you have put on Christ, then since you have the Son within you and have been made like to Him, you have been brought into one family with Him and into the same species (*idean*). . . . Do you see his insatiable soul? . . . [Paul] is not satisfied with the phrase ['You have put on Christ']; he explains it, and in doing so he describes a closer union still: 'You are all one person (*heis*) in Christ Jesus' (Gal. 3:28). That is to say, all of you have but one form, one character, which is Christ's. Could one find a more awesome declaration? He who just lately was but a Greek, or a Jew, or a slave, now goes about with the form, not of an angel or archangel, but of the very Lord of all things; in his own person he shows forth Christ.[24]

Augustine moves in much the same tradition, but with the nuances of his own approach. For him, all men are Adam, and Adam is all men. In Adam all men are guilty of disobedience, in him all are constituted sinners. From Adam all men have their life, and that life is defiled in its origin. This solidarity in sin God determined to counteract by another solidarity, a solidarity in good, a solidarity in Christ. He has chosen a new mass of men, the Body of the Saviour. How enter that Body? By a rebirth. For just as a human being comes to life by being born of man and woman, so one becomes a member of the Body of Christ by being reborn of God and the church. In a succinct expression: "When

[24] John Chrysostom, *Comm. in Gal.* 3, 5 (*PG* 61: 656).

you have been baptized, then you have been born members."[25]

Irenaeus and Hilary, Chrysostom and Augustine—these are examples which illustrate a tenacious patristic tradition: the individual is incorporated into Christ, becomes a member of his Body, begins to live his life, through baptism. But it would be historical myopia, a tragic misreading of the evidence, to see in the patristic conception of baptism, of incorporation into Christ, some sort of magical rite unrelated to the faith without which it is impossible to please God. For the Fathers, as for Paul, it is faith that is the beginning of justification; and this faith stems from God's gracious giving. To come to Christ is to be converted to Christ through faith.[26] The significance of faith emerges clearly and forcefully from a paragraph of Fulgentius of Ruspe:

[Paul says:] 'Without faith it is impossible to please God' (Heb. 11:6). The reason is, faith is the foundation of all blessings, faith is the beginning of man's salvation. Without it no one can belong to the number of God's children; for without it no one obtains the grace of justification in this world, and without it no one will possess life eternal in the world to come. . . . Without faith all effort of man is without value.[27]

In the same line of thought, it is instructive to read the

[25] Augustine, *Serm. Denis* 25, 8 (Morin, p. 164; *PL* 46: 940). The complete sentence is even richer: "Filii matris, quando baptizati estis, tunc membra Christi nata estis: adducite ad lavacrum baptismatis quos potestis, ut, sicut filii fuistis quando nati estis, sic etiam ducendo ad nascendum matres Christi esse possitis."
[26] Cf. Augustine, *Epist.* 194, 11-12 (*CSEL* 57, 185); *De gratia et lib. arb.* 10 (*PL* 44: 888); *Tract. in Ioan.* 26, 1 (*CCL* 36, 260).
[27] Fulgentius, *De fide, ad Petrum*, Prol. 1 (*PL* 65: 671).

liturgical literature of the early church, the rite of baptism. What is consistently demanded of the candidate is an affirmation of faith. Take Hippolytus' *Apostolic Tradition*, which provides such precious information about the liturgy in Rome in the early years of the third century:

And [when] he [who is to be baptized] goes down to the water, let him who baptizes lay hand on him saying thus: 'Dost thou believe in God the Father Almighty?' And he who is being baptized shall say: 'I believe.' Let him forthwith baptize him once, having his hand laid upon his head. And after [this] let him say: 'Dost thou believe in Christ Jesus, the Son of God, who was born of Holy Spirit and the Virgin Mary, who was crucified in the days of Pontius Pilate, and died, [and was buried] and rose the third day living from the dead and ascended into the heavens, and sat down at the right hand of the Father, and will come to judge the living and the dead?' And when he says: 'I believe,' let him baptize him the second time. And again let him say: 'Dost thou believe in the Holy Spirit in the holy Church, and the resurrection of the flesh?' And he who is being baptized shall say: 'I believe.' And so let him baptize him the third time.[28]

The baptism of which the Fathers speak, therefore, is the baptism of a believer, a human being who has accepted Christ in faith. And if we may apply to the Fathers in general what a contemporary scholar has shown of Hilary in particular, the faith in question "is not a cold, objective intellectualism, but is to be ani-

[28] Translation essentially from *The Treatise on the Apostolic Tradition of St. Hippolytus of Rome* 1, ed. G. Dix (London and New York, 1937), 36-37. Cf. also Justin Martyr, *Apol.* 1, 61 and 65 (*PG* 6: 420, 428).

mated by an active piety, a vital, loving union with divine truth which is embodied in Christ."[29]

But if it is true that patristic theology finds in the baptism of a believer incorporation into the Body of Christ, it remains equally true that, for the Fathers, the sacrament *par excellence* of unity, therefore *the* sacrament of the Body of Christ, is the Eucharist. The church is the Body of Christ because she lives by the body of Christ.

The texts are discouragingly many, impressively rich; I can do no more than touch the tradition by choice examples from East and West. Take Hilary of Poitiers, in the middle of the fourth century. The union of Christians in Christ, he insists, is more than a union of wills; it is a communication of divinity to men. And what is the agent of this divinization? Hilary's answer is highly realistic:

. . . Is Christ within us today by the truth of His nature or by harmony of will? If the Word has really become flesh, and if in the Lord's food we really receive the Word as flesh, how can anyone think that He does not abide in us by His nature (*naturaliter*)? For by being born man He has taken to Himself, beyond possibility of severance, the nature of our flesh, and has joined the nature of His flesh to His eternal nature beneath the mystery (*sub sacramento*) of the flesh that was to be imparted to us. This is why we are all one: because the Father is in Christ, and Christ is in us. . . . The Father in Christ and Christ in us make us to be one in them. If, therefore, Christ has really taken the flesh of our body, and if that man who was born of Mary is

[29] J. E. Emmenegger, *The Functions of Faith and Reason in the Theology of Saint Hilary of Poitiers* (Washington, D.C., 1947), p. 187.

really Christ, and if in the mystery (*sub mysterio*) we really receive the flesh of His body (and consequently we are one, because the Father is in Him and He is in us), how can one affirm a [mere] oneness of will, since the quality of His nature in the mystery is the mystery of perfect oneness?[30]

I do not hesitate to make my own the commentary of Mersch on the passage just translated; it recaptures Hilary's mind succinctly and masterfully: ". . . Christ is united with the Christians for two reasons: He has taken them all into Himself by His Incarnation and He comes into them all in the Eucharist. True, these two mystical interiorities are not on the same level. The first, which proceeds from the Incarnation, is the indispensable principle of the other. The second is simply the application to all men, the full realization, of the first. It is by coming into us in the Eucharist that Christ enables us to live that divine life which, by means of the Incarnation, He has brought to every man."[31]

As Hilary sees it, Christ has revealed clearly enough the steps in our progression towards perfect unity. These steps are discoverable in Jn. 14:20: "In that day you shall know that I am in the Father, and you in me, and I in you." Hilary's exegesis is swift and inflexible:

[What He means is that] He is in the Father by the nature

---

[30] Hilary of Poitiers, *De trinitate* 8, 13 (*PL* 10: 246). The tortuous final sentence of the passage here translated, particularly the compressed causal clause which closes it ("cum naturalis per sacramentum proprietas, perfectae sacramentum sit unitatis"), obscures somewhat the basically simple idea: through the flesh that the Word took from us in the Incarnation and communicates to us in the Eucharist, we are perfectly one in and with Christ, and through him with the Father.

[31] Mersch, *op. cit.*, pp. 302-303.

of the divinity, that we on our part are in Him by His birth in the body, and that we should believe He is in us by the sacramental mystery (*per sacramentorum mysterium*). In this way would we be taught the perfect oneness we have through the Mediator: while we abide in Him, He Himself abides in the Father; and while He abides in the Father, He abides in us. Thus would we progress to oneness with the Father, since we would be in Him [the Son] by nature, who is in the Father by nature on the level of generation, the while He [the Son] abides ever in us by His nature.[32]

Chrysostom's doctrine on the role of the Eucharist in the Body of Christ is quite the same as Hilary's, but it is wonderfully warm and personal; for he is not the theologian in the tower, but the preacher in the pulpit. This itself is not without significance: it means that in the age of the Fathers the thesis that *the* sacrament of the Body of Christ is the Eucharist was not so much a theory for theological speculation as a truth for Christian meditation. Chrysostom tells his congregation in Antioch:

That we may become [one body and members of His flesh and bones] not merely on the level of love but realistically (*kat' auto to pragma*) too, let us be mingled into that flesh. This is effected by means of the food which He has graciously given as proof of His love for us. For this reason has He mingled Himself with us and mixed His body in us, that we may really be some one thing, as a body united with its head. What ardent love this manifests![33]

There you have the basic principle: the purpose of the Eucharist is the unity of Christ's Body—through

[32] Hilary of Poitiers, *De trinitate* 8, 15 (*PL* 10: 248). The "sacramental mystery" here is surely the Eucharist.
[33] John Chrysostom, *Hom. in Ioan.* 46, 3 (*PG* 59: 260).

Christ's body. This principle takes on color and life, it throbs and thrills, when Chrysostom is explaining I Cor. 10:16: "The bread which we break, is it not communion in the body of Christ?"

Paul has just said 'communion (*koinōnia*) in the body of Christ.' But the communicant is distinct from that of which he communicates. Yet, even this distinction, slight as it may seem, Paul abolished. For, after saying 'communion in the body,' he sought to say something still more intimate, and so he added: 'Because the bread is one, we many are one body' (I Cor. 10:17). Why, he says, do I speak of communion? We *are* that very body. For what is the bread? The body of Christ. And what do they become who partake of it? The body of Christ. Not many bodies, but one body. For just as the bread consists of many grains, so united that they are no longer distinguishable, but they still subsist, though their individuality is no longer apparent to the eye because of their union, so are we united one with the other and with Christ. For you are not fed on one body and he on a different body, but we are all fed on the same. . . .[34]

A breathtaking insight, from Paul to Chrysostom: one sacramental body of Christ, *therefore* one Mystical Body of Christ. The church is the Body of Christ because she lives by the body of Christ.

This doctrine touches new heights in Cyril of Alexandria. Careful theologian, especially anxious in his *Commentary on John* to uncover the dogmatic sense of the text, Cyril argues that the flesh of Christ not only gives life to the individual Christian; it gives unity

[34] John Chrysostom, *Hom. in 1 Cor.* 24, 2 (*PG* 61: 200). To preserve the flavor of the original and the consistent use of *koinōnia* and *koinōneō*, I have used "communicate" in the archaic sense of "participate."

to the whole Christian body. I quote only one of many magnificent passages:

> By one body—I mean His own—[Christ] blesses (*eulogōn*), through the mystical participation, those who believe in Him, and in this way He makes them concorporate (*syssōmous*) with Himself and with one another. . . . For if 'we all partake of the one bread' (I Cor. 10:17), we are all made one body, since Christ cannot be divided. For this reason has the church been called the Body of Christ, and we His individual members, as Paul observed.[35]

About the same time that Cyril was trumpeting this thesis in the East, Augustine was preaching it in the West. For him, as Mersch observes, "the Eucharist is not simply the sacrament of the Real Presence. . . . It is the sacred sign or sacrament of the unity of the Church; it is the sacrament of the Mystical Body."[36] Augustine tells his neophytes that the priest at Communion reveals what they are when he says: "The body of Christ." To which they answer "Amen"; they subscribe to his statement. And Augustine goes on:

> . . . What is that one bread [of which Paul spoke]? 'We many are one body' (I Cor. 10:17). Remember, bread is not made of one grain, but of many. When exorcized, you were as if ground in a mill. When baptized, you were as if besprinkled. When you received the fire of the Holy Spirit, you were as if baked. Be what you see, and receive what you are. . . . Though [the Apostle] did not say what we were to understand of the chalice, his meaning is sufficiently clear. . . . Recall, my brothers, how wine is made. Many grapes hang on the cluster, but the juice of [all] the

[35] Cyril of Alexandria, *Comm. in Ioan.* 11, 11 (Pusey 2, 735).
[36] Mersch, *op. cit.*, p. 348.

grapes is mingled together in oneness. Thus did the Lord
Christ signify us, will that we should belong to Him, con-
secrate on His table the mystery of our peace and unity.[37]

In summary, then: we are confronted with a twin tradition. On the one hand, the believer is incorporated
into Christ, becomes a member of his Body, begins to
live his life, through baptism. On the other hand, the
sacrament *par excellence* of unity, therefore *the* sacrament of the Body of Christ, is the Eucharist.

There is no contradiction here; quite the contrary.
There are insights here—at least two fine insights.
One is—at any rate, for contemporary theology—fairly
obvious. I mean the realization that baptism is but a
beginning; that incorporation into Christ, remarkable
gift though it is, does not automatically guarantee the
full richness of divine life; that the life which has its
birth in belief and in baptism must be nourished if it is
to grow and flower; that the very unity of Christ's
Body is imperiled to the extent that the life of the
members is impoverished; and that the sacrament of
growth, building on belief and on baptism, is the sacrament which gives us Christ himself for our food and
drink.[38]

The second insight is more subtle. Its background is an
awareness of the fact that the meeting ground between
God and man is the humanity of Christ. Through the
Incarnation humanity comes into contact with the

[37] Augustine, *Serm.* 272 (*PL* 38: 1247-1248).
[38] In this connection, it is instructive to see how the Eucharist,
not baptism, is at the center of St. Thomas' thought on membership in the church; cf. C. E. O'Neill, "Members of the
Church: *Mystici corporis* and St. Thomas," *American Ecclesias-
tical Review*, CXLVIII (1963), 180-182.

humanity of Christ; through his humanity it comes into contact with his divinity; through his divinity it comes to share in the life of the Trinity.

The patristic insight builds on this awareness. It sees in the Eucharist a distinctive prolongation of the Incarnation; for in Communion man touches in unique fashion the humanity of Christ, his flesh and blood, and through this contact with the life-giving body of Christ participates in his divinity.[39]

In the patristic understanding of the Body of Christ, the Eucharist is the consummation of the Incarnation. What the material body of Christ initiated in the Incarnation, the sacramental body of Christ completes in the Eucharist: the oneness of men with God and with one another in the humanity of Christ.

III LOVE

For the Fathers, the Body of Christ is not merely a doctrine to be studied, or even an organism to be in; it is a life to be lived. In the hands of the Fathers, no doctrine stays sterile. They would have subscribed warmly to the remarkable affirmation of St. Thomas: "There are two ways of desiring knowledge. One way of desiring knowledge is to desire it as a perfection of one's self; and that is the way philosophers desire it. The other way of desiring knowledge is to desire it, not as a perfection of one's self, but because through this knowl-

[39] Cf. L. Janssens, "Notre filiation divine d'après saint Cyrille d'Alexandrie," *Ephemerides theologicae Lovanienses*, XV (1938), 253.

edge the one we love becomes present to us; and that is the way saints desire it."

"Through this knowledge the one we love becomes present to us." This is peculiarly true of Body-of-Christ doctrine as the Fathers of the church teach it and preach it. The Eucharist, consummating the Incarnation, is seen as the realization of Christian fraternal love. In the common participation of all believers, without exception or discrimination, in one table, the Eucharist represents and demands an extraordinary love.

The tradition is as ancient as Ignatius of Antioch. His is a theology of unity: one God, one Christ, one Christian body, one Eucharist, one love. In the eyes of Ignatius, Christ is not truly ours, and we are not genuinely Christians, unless we have one prayer, one mind, one hope, one love—in brief, one Christ.[40]

This tradition could be traced out in impressive detail; for patristic theology never wearies of insisting that the oneness between God and man in Christ that had its inception in the Incarnation, and has its consummation in the Eucharist, must work itself out in a love that is limitless, a love that is all-inclusive, a love that is commanded and justified by the profoundly simple fact that the one I love is Christ.

The tradition is long and impressive; but, for our immediate purpose, I shall concentrate on two remarkable preachers: Chrysostom in the East, Augustine in the

[40] Cf. e.g., Ignatius of Antioch, *Ad Magnesios* 6, 2; 7, 1-2 (Funk-Bihlmeyer, p. 90). See also the splendid treatment of Ignatius' doctrine on unity by P. Th. Camelot, in his Introduction to the Letters of Ignatius in *Sources chrétiennes* 10 (3rd ed.; Paris, 1958), 20-55, esp. 52-55 on the Eucharist as sacrament of unity.

West. If you would see Body-of-Christ doctrine
brought down to earth, read Chrysostom. Strange
though it seems, read him on almsgiving. Rarely has a
preacher urged almsgiving so incessantly; rarely has
a preacher associated almsgiving so intimately and so
compellingly with our incorporation in Christ. His
most forceful argument is the mystical identity of the
poor with Jesus; his favorite text, "As long as you did
it to one of these my least brethren, you did it to me"
(Matt. 25:40).

To begin with, the basic doctrine comes through with
lucid clarity:

. . . we refuse to feed [Jesus] when He is hungry, to clothe
Him when He is naked; when we see Him begging alms, we
pass Him by. Oh, no doubt, if you were to see Him in person, each of you would empty out all he has. But, right
now this man is Christ; for He Himself said: 'It is I.' Why,
then, do you not empty on him all you have?[41]

This doctrine, that we are Christ, is so intimate a part
of him that Chrysostom's pleas for the poor are im-
passioned. Because the poor are Christ, they take
precedence over church ornaments:

What is the use of loading [Christ's] table with cups of
gold, if He Himself is perishing from hunger? First satisfy
His hunger; then adorn His table with what remains. . . . I
am not saying this to put an end to such munificence. I am
urging you to do the one *and* the other—more accurately,
to do the one *before* the other.[42]

At times he seems haunted by his vision of a homeless

[41] John Chrysostom, *Hom. in Matt.* 88, 3 (*PG* 58: 778).
[42] *Ibid.* 50, 4 (*PG* 58: 509).

Christ, a hungry Christ, a naked Christ. He puts moving words in the mouth of Christ:

... it is such a slight thing I beg ... nothing very expensive ... bread, a roof, words of comfort. [If the rewards I promised hold no appeal for you] then show at least a natural compassion when you see me naked, and remember the nakedness I endured for you on the Cross. . . . I fasted for you then, and I suffer hunger for you now; I was thirsty when I hung on the Cross, and I thirst still in the poor, in both ways to draw you to myself and to make you humane for your own salvation. . . . I do not say 'Deliver me from poverty,' or, 'Give me riches'. . . . I do ask, however, bread, a cloak, some little relief from my hunger. If I am thrown into prison, I do not compel you to loose my chains and set me free; I ask only that you come and see me who am in chains for you. This favor is enough for me, and for it alone I give you heaven. . . .[43]

One passage more than all others has stirred me profoundly. The poor in the public square remind Chrysostom of an altar ready for sacrifice; and he proceeds to show that the poor are more venerable an altar than the altar of stone on which the Sacrifice is offered, on which the body of Christ rests:

This altar is composed of the very members of Christ, and the Lord's Body becomes an altar for you. This venerate: in the flesh you are offering the Lord's victim. This altar is more awesome than the altar in this church—not only more awesome than the altar of the Old Testament. Do not be troubled! You see, this altar [in the church] is a wondrous thing because of the Victim that has been placed thereon; but that altar, the altar of the compassionate man, is won-

[43] John Chrysostom, *Hom. in Rom.* 15, 6 (*PG* 60: 547-548).

drous not simply for the same reason, but also because it is composed of the very Victim that makes this altar. Again, the former is a wondrous thing in that, though made of stone, it becomes holy because it receives the body of Christ; the latter, because it *is* the Body of Christ. Therefore, it is more awesome than the altar near which you, a layman, are standing. . . . This altar you can see set up everywhere, in the lane and in the market, and at any hour you may sacrifice thereon; for here too sacrifice is consummated.[44]

Thus far Chrysostom, apostle of the poor, because the poor are Christ; apostle of love, because love is intertwined with Christ's body—with the body he took from us in the Incarnation, with the Body he fashioned from his lanced side on Calvary, with the body he gives us for our food in the Eucharist.

Augustine is far more a theologian than Chrysostom. Still, like Chrysostom, he is very much a preacher. As pastor, his first care is for the union of Christ and all Christendom; his ceaseless concern is for Christian charity. The union and the charity he seeks have for doctrinal basis the mystery of charity in the mystery of unity. In a single sentence of Augustine: "This man is men, and men are this man; for many are one, since Christ is one."[45] Mersch has, I think, recaptured Augustine's mind and approach admirably:

He repeats over and over again that charity is something essential to the Mystical Body. Charity is its first principle, for it owes its very existence to the divine love that has united us all with His Incarnate Son. Charity is also its first

[44] John Chrysostom, *Hom. in 2 Cor.* 20, 3 (*PG* 61: 540).
[45] Augustine, *In ps.* 127, 14 (*PL* 37: 1686).

consequence, for our union with God and with our fellow men gives rise in us to both the exigency and the power to love God and our brethren with a new, theological love. When this love meets and unites with the divine love . . . it becomes the principle of a more intimate union. This latter union now calls for and excites a more intense love, which in turn leads to a union still more profound. In this way do charity and unity beget and intensify each other. . . .[46]

Several facets of Augustine's doctrine and preaching in this direction merit special attention. First, he sees this unity as so remarkably real that even God cannot separate the two he has joined together: to love Christ completely, he must love all of us:

[God,] who loves His Son, cannot do otherwise than love the members of His Son. Nor has He any other reason for loving His Son's members except that He loves Him. . . . The love wherewith the Father loves the Son is also in us. How? Because we are the members of the Son, and because we are loved in Him when He is loved wholly, that is, Head and body.[47]

Second, our love should be utterly catholic: it should be offered, as the grace of God is offered, to all:

Love all men, even your enemies; love them, not because they are your brothers, but that they may become your brothers—so that you may ever burn with brotherly love, whether for him who is already your brother, or for your enemy, that he may by [your] loving become your brother. . . . Even he who does not yet believe in Christ . . . love him, and love him with brotherly love. He is not yet your brother, but you love him precisely that he may be your

[46] Mersch, op. cit., p. 434.
[47] Augustine, Tract. in Ioan. 110, 5; 111, 6 (CCL 36, 626, 632).

brother. All our love, therefore, is brotherly love towards Christians, towards all Christ's members.[48]

Some, Augustine sorrows, "would limit love to the land of Africa!" No, he protests: "Extend your love over the entire earth, if you would love Christ; for the members of Christ lie all over the earth." Then an interesting argumentation: "If you love [only] a part, you are divided; if you are divided, you are not in the Body; if you are not in the Body, you are not under the Head." Then a strong observation: "What is the use of believing, if you blaspheme? You adore Him in the Head, you blaspheme Him in the Body. He loves His Body. . . ."[49]

Even more impressively Augustine asserts:

. . . the children of God are the Body of the only Son of God, and since He is the Head and we the members, there is but one Son of God. Therefore, he that loves the children of God loves the Son of God, and he that loves the Son of God loves the Father. Nor can anyone love the Father if he does not love the Son; and he that loves the Son loves also the children of God. What children of God? The members of the Son of God. And by loving he too becomes a member; through love he enters into the structure of the Body of Christ. And there shall be one Christ loving Himself (*unus Christus amans seipsum*). For when the members love one another, the Body loves itself.[50]

[48] Augustine, *In epist. Ioan. ad Parthos* 10, 7 (*PL* 35: 2059). The final sentence in the Latin is ambiguous, dependent for its precise meaning on where one pauses or punctuates: "Ergo tota dilectio nostra fraterna est erga christianos, erga omnia membra eius."
[49] *Ibid.* 10, 8 (*PL* 35: 2060).
[50] *Ibid.* 10, 3 (*PL* 35: 2055).

On this aspect of the Body of Christ, Augustine has a powerful short sentence: "Love cannot be divided."[51] Love the children of God, and you love the Son of God; love the Son of God, and you love the Father. Conversely, you dare not say, you cannot say, that you love Christ, if you love not the members of Christ—all his members, without exception, without discrimination.

This, in the patristic understanding of Christ, is an inescapable conclusion. Incarnation, Eucharist, love: this *is* the Body of Christ. *Unus Christus amans seipsum.*

[51] *Ibid.* 10, 3 (*PL* 35: 2056).

ROMAN CATHOLIC INSIGHTS:

A CONCEPT OF THE BODY
OF CHRIST IN CONTEMPORARY
ROMAN CATHOLIC THEOLOGY

BERNARD COOKE, S. J.

The Body of Christ,
Catholic Theological View

It seems to me that the sequence of papers presented today could give a certain subtle impression that would be quite erroneous, namely that the previous papers of Father Ahern and Father Burghardt deal with the past state of belief concerning the church as body of Christ, whereas I, on the contrary, will deal with contemporary theologizing on that subject. Actually, the papers presented by these two men are excellent examples of what is, to my mind at least, the most important area of present-day Catholic theologizing about the church, the scholarly effort to appraise with understanding and objectivity the early sources of our Christian faith. It is precisely this return to the sources by biblical and patristics scholars that has contributed so importantly to the contemporary revitalization of theology.[1]

[1] For a brief analysis of the impact of biblical and patristic studies on present-day Catholic theology, cf. R. Aubert, *La thé-ologie catholique au milieu du XXè siècle* (Paris, 1954), chaps. 1 and 2.

My effort, then, will be to give some idea of current trends in what one might call—though the term is not totally satisfactory—the dogmatic theology of the church as body of Christ.

No documentation would be required to substantiate the statement that Catholic theology of the church has entered upon a new epoch in our own day; and that which is characteristic of this new period of ecclesiology is the approach to the church as mystery, as the body of Christ.[2] It is true that some better treatments of the church in the nineteenth and early twentieth century—like those of Moehler, Franzelin, and Schrader[3]—do contain an important discussion of the church as the mystical body. However, even in such theologians it is the structural aspect of the church that, for apologetic reasons, receives the bulk of attention; among lesser theologians and in many standard manuals of theology one will search to find more than a passing mention of the church as mystery. Though one deplores this aridity which crept into the classic modern tract "de ecclesia", it is somewhat understandable when one examines the rather adverse conditions in which this tract developed. As far back as the *De regimine christiano* of Jacques of Viterbo, written in answer to Philip the Fair, and the *Summa de ecclesia*

---

[2] On the shift in Catholic ecclesiology, cf. G. Weigel, "The Present State of Catholic Ecclesiology", *Proceedings of the Society of Catholic College Teachers of Sacred Doctrine*, VII (1961), 21-31.

[3] C. Schrader, *De unitate Romana* (1862-1866); J. B. Franzelin, *Theses de Ecclesia* (1887); J. A. Moehler, *Die Einheit in der Kirche* (1825), *Symbolik* (1832). See also the discussion of H. de Lubac in his *Splendour of the Church* (New York, 1956), pp. 61-63.

of Torquemada (fifteenth century) one finds the explanation of the church's reality and role described in
a controversial context; and this is certainly not less
true of Bellarmine and the other Catholic theologians
whose works on the church are directed against the
positions of the reformers. Add to this the natural in-
crease in interest in the institutional aspects of the
church which came with the ascendancy of canon law
towards the end of the Middle Ages and thereafter;
further complicate the picture with the increasing loss
of the sense of mystery in the sacraments; and the
results which history presents us are not a surprise.[4]

To those raised on this organizational understanding
of the church (and though their ranks are somewhat
thinning, they are still numerous) the increasing mention of the church as the mystical body of Christ has
been looked on as a dubious trend in Catholic theology.
Indeed, in the early stages of return to this notion of
the church there were some exaggerated ideas, or at
least expressions, that tended towards a mystic pan-
theism; against such, portions of the encyclical letter
of Pius XII on the mystical body are directed. Ad-
mittedly, too, there is a great deal of vague thinking
about this deeper mystery reality of the church,
occasioned to some extent perhaps, by the use of the
term "mystical" along with body of Christ.

As studies like those of Father de Lubac have clarified for us, this term "mystical body" actually has a
Eucharistic origin, and by a most interesting transfer
of terms came to be applied to the church.[5] In its cur-

[4] Cf. G. Weigel, *op. cit.*, pp. 23-24.
[5] See H. de Lubac, *Corpus Mysticum, l'Eucharistie et l'Eglise au
Moyen Age* (Paris, 1949).

rent Catholic theological usage the term has been applied to the church as body of Christ to indicate that there is a unity deeper than an ordinary moral or societal unity, but which does not lessen the distinctive individuality of the members of the church.[6] Perhaps if we regain some of the earlier awareness of the interlacing of the mysteries of church and Eucharist, we will understand the church as mystical body with increased reference to the mysteries, the sacraments, which are the church's life actions.[7]

Our present task, however, is not to suggest lines of development for the future but to examine the present Catholic theological understanding of the church as the body of Christ. To this purpose I propose to discuss five facets of this mystery: (1) The church is the manifestation of Christ as life-giving spirit. (2) The church is the instrument for Christ's continuing redemptive activity in human history. (3) The church's unity comes in the common life of faith in Christ and love of him. (4) The church is the extension, ground, and result of the Eucharistic mystery. (5) The church as manifestation and instrument of Christ is so socially; that which faith and the Eucharist form is a true society.

Church Manifests Christ as Living Spirit — Quite obviously, the discussion of the church manifesting Christ

[6] Cf. J. Salaverri, *Sacrae Theologiae Summa*, vol. I (Madrid, 1952), 818-819; also the encyclical "Mystici Corporis", *AAS* XXXV (1943), 199, 221.

[7] One of the finest contributions on this topic is K. Rahner's essay "Wort und Eucharistie" in *Aktuelle Fragen zur Eucharistie* (Munich, 1960).

as living spirit brings us into intimate contact with the present-day theologizing about the resurrection of Jesus.[8]

For Christians of differing confessions the resurrection of Jesus occupies the position of the key event in the establishment of the mystery of Christianity. To a Catholic theologian this event is much more than the awakening of faith in the early church to the redemptive significance of the death of Jesus. Rather, Catholic belief is that in his resurrection Jesus of Nazareth enters into a new way of life, one in which his corporeal existence is subsumed into a new human way of living, which is dominated by spirit. Christ received the fulfillment of divine action in his humanity so that now he can be called a living spirit, dominated by the lifegiving power of the third person of the Blessed Trinity.[9]

This new way of life, no longer confined by the limitations of our space and time, enables Christ to be present to men of every place and every age; but in a sense it also removes him from immediate manifestation of himself within the ordinary human context of history. Whereas our bodies in this present life act as that which locates and manifests our own personal spiritual being to the men who surround us and brings us into contact with the material things of this world, the new and glorified body of Christ does not function properly in this way. This role of being the external manifestation of the vivifying presence of Christ among men is

[8] Probably the most important book in drawing recent theology to discussing the resurrection is F. X. Durrwell, *The Resurrection* (New York, 1960).
[9] Cf. Durrwell, *op. cit.*, chaps. 3 and 4.

now assumed by the Christian community; and in assuming this role it acts truly as body of Christ. "Where two or three are gathered together in my name, there I am in the midst of them."

Where the members of the community of faith in Christ, the members of his church, are gathered, one can know that there is a presence of Christ, for this is a portion of his church, his body. Just as the pages of the New Testament point to the fact that Jesus of Nazareth is the dwelling place of the spirit of God, the spirit who is already described as overshadowing Mary at the incarnation and who manifests his presence as Christ begins his public ministry in the scene of the baptism. This spirit Christ sends into his church as its vivifying and unifying principle in the mystery of Pentecost. The church is Christ's body because it is the dwelling place of his spirit. It has a common life, it has an organic unity, because this spirit pervades it, communicating to it the very life possessed by Christ himself in the mystery of the resurrection.[10]

Risen triumphant after conflict with death itself, Christ entered upon the full dominion of human history which is his right as the incarnate word of God. However, this dominion of Christ, functioning in the area of mystery and transcendence, must find expression in the lives and history of men. It is the church which acts as the means of transmitting this dominion of Christ into the lives of men; a dominion not of domination

[10] This idea dominates the book of Y. Congar, *The Mystery of the Church* (Baltimore, 1960), which begins with a treatment of Pentecost and continues with an emphasis on the role of the Spirit in the Church; cf. also L. Cerfaux, *The Church in the Theology of St. Paul* (New York, 1959), pp. 172-175, 232-236.

but of love, which points to the fact that the church's manifestation of Christ must be one governed by the mystery of Christian love.

Even prior to his death and resurrection Jesus of Nazareth quite clearly acted against the mystery of evil and death; and he manifested this fact in those striking actions we call his signs, his miracles. In these miracles it is quite obvious that the internal life-giving force and intent of Jesus is translated into the external sphere of human living by his voice and his hands. How often Christ says, "Take up your bed and walk," or "Lazarus, come forth!" How often also the gesture of the extended hand or the touch of Christ was the instrument for the power of his theandric action, passing in a life-giving flow to the cure of those who were afflicted either by physical or moral evil.

With the mystery of the resurrection Christ remains active in human history. This life-giving power of his abides with men to redeem them, and the manifestation of this consoling fact is the existence among men of his church which now, as his body, makes him present to men. It is the organ through which he can speak, through whose hands he can act. The church bespeaks the dwelling of God among men as surely as did the presence of Christ's own historical body in Palestine of 2000 years ago. It is a continuation of the mystery of his replacement of the Jerusalem temple as the abode of Jahweh.[11]

Catholic theology, then, does not see Christ in his risen state as identical with that body which is the church;

[11] Cf. chaps. 6 and 7 in Y. Congar, *The Mystery of the Temple* (Westminster, Md., 1961).

rather Christ himself has passed from the historical manner of his previous existing into completion of life in which body and soul are transformed into full spiritual being. Yet the church actually does function as his body in that it makes him present. It locates and manifests him, reveals the abiding presence of his redeeming power to a world which cannot perceive his spiritual being.

The Church, Instrument of Christ's Continuing Redemptive Activity — Actually we have already been dealing to some extent with this second topic as we spoke of the church as manifesting Christ in history; but now we can approach more formally the idea that the church is the instrument through which Christ's continuing redemptive activity is effected. Christians who accept the redemptive power of Christ's suffering, death, and resurrection are all agreed upon the uniqueness of the happening which then occurred, agreed also upon the completeness and adequacy of the action performed by Jesus of Nazareth in so redeeming mankind. There can be no question but what one must remain fully conscious of the *hapax* which the New Testament literature employs to describe these redemptive acts. They are a 'once for all' in human history, a summit never before or never since attained. It is they and they alone which dominate all human existing and offer the ground and the hope of human salvation.

Yet those who accept the manifest uniqueness of this act differ with regard to the role of the church as it lives out the centuries consequent upon the death and resurrection of Christ. Is the role of the church simply to be a place where this unique act is recalled and faith in it instilled, or does the church itself enter somehow into a continuing dynamic presence of Christ in these redeeming mysteries? Catholic theology opts for the second of these two positions and sees the church in human history as that through which and in which Christ continues to transform the world by continuing the acts begun 2000 years ago. For the Catholic theologian there is no question of the church adding something to the work of Christ which that work itself does not contain in a sense already. There can be no implication that Christ did not do enough and that somehow the church must add to what he did.[12] Yet the fact remains that the redeeming power of Christ is meant to touch men of every age and situation of life, and that this process of the actual effecting of the work of redemption in human beings and their actions and their lives is carried out through the medium of the words and the acts of the church. At the heart of this redeeming transforming activity lie the grace and the love and the intent of Christ which were themselves the heart of that action which began in the Cenacle and continued through Calvary and into the Easter mystery; but this intent is translated in history in the speech and gestures of the Christian community.

Again we note how this is like, by way of analogy, to the function of our own bodies as instruments of our human intention. All our human activity, when it is deeply personal, proceeds from our consciousness, our

[12] The Council of Trent in its twenty-second session, while stressing the efficacy of the Mass, makes clear the fact that this in no way detracts from the sacrifice of the cross; cf. *The Church Teaches*, 749, 759.

love, our motivations, our free choice, and our intention to effect some particular goal. Yet it is not sufficient for us merely to intend, merely to wish to do
something, or even to decide it. This intent must then
find expression, must be translated, through those powers possessed by our bodies and controlled by our
spirit. Thus our spiritual being is able to find expression
in the corporeaľ realities of the world which surrounds
us. Even our effecting of spiritual change in the consciousness and affectivity of our fellow human beings
must pass through the channel of our bodily activity.
So, throughout human history, the risen Christ, living
spirit that he is, source of the transforming power
of human history, uses the corporeal reality of the
Christian community to transmit to human lives and
human institutions the transforming power of his
risen life.[13] In this way, Christ truly uses the church as
his body.

This active relationship of Christ to his church, this
contribution which the church makes by being the
instrument of Christ, come to fullest expression in
those highly significant actions in the church's life
which we call the sacraments.[14] Functioning not primarily in terms of the physical forces which are exerted
in any given sacramental action, but rather in terms of
the meaning or significance which these acts contain,
the sacraments truly contribute—not by themselves but

[13] Cf. Durrwell, *op. cit.*, chaps. 7 and 8; also A. Feuillet, "Le
temps de l'Eglise d'après le quatrième Evangile et l'Apocalypse",
Maison-Dieu, LXV (1961), 60-79.
[14] Cf. B. Cooke, "The Sacraments as the Continuing Acts of
Christ", *Proceedings of the Catholic Theological Society of
America*, XVI (1961), 43-68.

as instruments of Christ—to that transformation of human lives which is Christ's redeeming work in human life. Sacraments not only recall the fact of Christ's redeeming acts of 2000 years ago; in these sacraments Christ himself continues to act, and they form as it were the external constituent of his continuing redeeming activity. Through them Christ continues to speak, continues to express sacrificially and effectively that acceptance of his Father's will which is the source of our salvation.

The Church Lives by Faith in Christ, by Love of Christ — When one speaks of body, one is speaking of that which possesses life and, because living, is a unity, not of completely univocal life expression, but of life which finds differing expression in different portions of the body and can therefore be called organic. Both the figure of vine used in John 15 and that of body employed in the Pauline literature point to the fact that the church is somehow or other such a unified reality, a living, vital, organic thing, one because there is one same life which courses throughout it. However, it would be naive and crass to conceive the life unity of the church of Christ as being something in the biological order; quite clearly there is something transcendent, something which has to do with the order of faith.[15]

[15]It is instructive to compare the view of L. Cerfaux, who in his books *The Church in the Theology of St. Paul* and *Christ in the Theology of St. Paul* (New York, 1959) is almost excessively wary of the idea of vital unity in the Church, and that of A. Wikenhauser in his *Pauline Mysticism* (New York, 1960), where the objective union of Christian with Christ is stressed.

Yet the life of the body of Christ which is the church is a mysterious reality. It should not be thought of as something apart from the mystery of Christianity. Again the word "mystical" has at times been misleading: it is not too unusual to find Catholics whose ideas with regard to this reality have not clarified, who think that there is some completely unknown mysterious force which binds the church together, and who forget that that of which scripture itself and the traditional teaching of the church speak is the life of faith and the life of charity. The church is one because it has one Lord, because it has one spirit, and one baptism. The church is one because it professes faith in this Lord; and the life of this community which is the church, that which its members share, a truly vital function— is the life of faith. To know, to love, are the highest activities of man as living, and the highest kind of personal consciousness known to man in that which has to do with the highest reality, the divine mystery revealed by God in and through Christ. Hence it is that the church truly lives a common life of faith-consciousness. This life is further unified by the object of faith which is the Father revealed in the mystery of Christ; this life is expressed by the church in the profession of faith, above all in the Christian sacraments.[16]

Not only does this common life of faith bind Christians together in the mystery of the church so that one spirit, one point of view, one outlook on life, unites them; but this life of faith is also a unity between Christ and his members. Faith is not simply a blind

[16] Cf. K. Rahner, "Wort und Eucharistie," cited in n. 7.

acceptance without understanding of something which is given authoritatively to men to accept; faith involves an understanding, a point of view, and this point of view is one that is given to man in the revelation in Christ. [Those who share the life of faith share Christ's own point of view which is communicated to them from him; therefore a profound unity of consciousness is shared by Christ and those who are the members of his church.]

Personal life, however, is not exhausted in consciousness. Persons are by the very nature of their being related beings; that is to say, persons are directed toward others in openness as expressed in love. So also the community of the faithful is a community united in this Spirit who causes in their hearts the love of Christ himself.[17] This love is twofold, at least in its expression. It is a love which unites Christians together because they share a common bond of affection for Christ who is their redeemer and Lord. It is also a bond of love for one another based upon their common love of Christ. In this second facet of the love which exists in the church one can see that the members of Christ share that very same love of mankind which Christ himself possesses and which lies at the heart of his redeeming action. It is Christ's human love, expressing as it does the divine love which is an even deeper mystery, which acts to transform and to redeem the world of men. Christians sharing this love of Christ are united with him and so, derivatively but truly, share in that stream

[17] Two recent studies on the N.T. view of charity and its role in the Christian community are those of V. Warnach, *Agape* (Duesseldorf, 1951), and C. Spicq, *Agapé dans le Nouveau Testament* (Paris, 1958-1959).

of redemptive power which causes the salvation of human history. The church as the body of Christ is joined with him in his love and his redemption, and is joined to him by its conscious acceptance of him in faith. Thus the Church is a living reality; it has a life, highly personal though somewhat mysterious. This life proceeds from the living spirit within it, the spirit who leads Christians to that commitment to Christ which is faith and to the love which results from it, for he is the spirit of love.

The Church Is the Extension, the Ground, and the Result of the Eucharistic Mystery — It may sound rather contradictory to say that the church, the body of Christ, is at one and the same time the *ground* of the Eucharistic action and the *result* of this action. Yet such is the case because of the vital reality of the church. Were it not for the fact that the church is the living body of Christ, the manifestation of his revealing action, the instrument of his redemptive work, the sacramental action of the Eucharist as seen by Catholic belief, would not be sacramental, but magical. It is only because of the abiding presence of the living, working Christ in its midst that the church can pretend to perform an action which is the continuation of Christ's own redeeming act and action; an action which, while it does not add to the intrinsic depth or worth of what Christ is doing, does still in mysterious fashion enter into the effecting of man's salvation.[18] If the Eucharist

[18] One of the most influential books in calling attention to the active presence of Christ in the sacraments is Père Roguet's little volume, *Christ Acts through the Sacraments* (Collegeville,

is a conjoined action of Christ and of those who form his body, it is so only because of the profound unity of life which that church shares from its divine master. Thus the mystery of the church as the body of Christ is that alone which gives full scope and meaning to the continuing enactment of that action commenced by Christ at the supper 2000 years ago.

On the other hand, this body which is the Church lives from this action of the Eucharist. The centuries-long tradition of Catholic thought has seen the external symbolic actions of the Lord's supper performed by the Christian community as a sign, not just of a continuing abiding presence of the historical Jesus in history, but of that other body which is the church. The very action of sacrifice performed by the community in union with Christ points externally to that unification of mind and heart which the community is here expressing. Communion in the body of Christ indicates that if a life is shared by this community, it is because of Christ's action in giving himself body and living spirit to this community which is his. It is not accidental that the external forms of the Eucharistic action involve food and drink, for these are signs of life. Symbolically and yet truly, this communion in the body and the blood of Christ is a life-giving force to the Christian community; from it flows that life of faith and love which we have already described.

The church is no source of life apart from the Lord who lives in its midst, apart from the Spirit he sends to abide in the Church. At the root of this life-giving

1954); cf. also E. Masure, *The Sacrifice of the Mystical Body* (London, 1954).

influence of Christ lie the great redemptive mysteries, the supper, death, and resurrection. These and these alone are the root of man's salvation; yet as Catholic faith and theology see it, these mysteries are precisely that which is re-presented in the Eucharistic action of the Mass.[19] By way of continuation rather than repetition, Christ still enacts that which he began 2000 years ago and which will continue unbroken and salvific until the final moments of human history. Thus the church is Eucharistic body, not in the sense that it is to be identified with the glorified body of Christ which is involved in the Eucharistic action, but rather that it is a body which lives from the Eucharist and finds its own highest vital expression in this action.

In addition to being the ground and the result of the Eucharistic mystery, the church as the body of Christ is also the extension of this mystery. Compressed into the Eucharistic act is the entirety of the salvific reality and significance of Christ's redeeming acts. It is here that in Christ himself and in his church is found the highest fulfillment of the triple office which Christ exercises as prophet, priest and king. Yet this power, this exercise of messianic office, is meant to flow out into the actual transformation of men; this the church does, grounding its action in the Eucharist. In the daily events of life, Christians must go out to witness to that truth revealed in and through Christ, must bring into a world which knows not Christ the rule of his love, and must by their own sanctity, charity, faith, extend the

[19] Though it is a little out of date, one of the best surveys of contemporary discussion on the manner of this Eucharistic representation is T. Filthaut's volume, *La théologie des mystères* (Paris, 1954).

priestly action of Christ into the Christian transformation of a world. The Eucharist points to the unification
of all mankind in Christ and through him to the Father.
It is the function of the church as Christ's body to
manifest this reality throughout all the spheres of
human activity and to achieve in the long and difficult
course of human history that gradual transformation
of a world until all things are caught up into Christ.
In this fashion, the total life of the church is meant to
embody that central life-giving force and significance
which is expressed in the Eucharistic action.

*The Church, the Body of Christ, Is a Society Formed
by Eucharist and Faith* — In this final point which we
wish to discuss, though we will be somewhat repeating
material already mentioned, we wish to draw attention
to the fact that the church is a society.[20] We have said
that it is a community, that it shares a common point of
view, that it is bound together by that love which
comes from Christ, a vital force operating on the highest level of human living. We have seen that this
church expresses its worship of the Father in and
through Christ in a communal action, in that action of
Eucharistic sacrifice which is the very source of its life.
Now we wish to stress the fact that this vital, unified
reality is truly a society. It is not that Christ simply
lives on in a large number of individuals, but that this
life possessed by the individuals is a true corporate
reality. Christianity is not a process of men achieving
their own salvation and working for the redemption

[20] For a detailed theological analysis of the church as society,
cf. C. Journet, *The Church of the Word Incarnate*, vol. I (New
York, 1954).

of others in an individualistic fashion. As Christians we are saved together and we enter together into the task of working with Christ for the salvation of the world.

If this church, this body of Christ, is a society, then it must necessarily (so it seems to Catholic theology) be involved visibly in the life of men. While it retains all the flexibility of its inner life of the spirit and of love, it must as society possess organization and therefore authority. This authority, Christ himself points to when he gives to his apostles a kingdom. It is an authority quite clearly to be exercised in the realm of the spirit, an authority which is commensurate with the objectives of the church, and an authority which in achieving these objectives must utilize those means proper to the nature of his church. Still, with all its flexibility, we must remember that an organizational aspect is of the very essence of the church as society. It is in this context that Catholic theology in its contemporary speculations would situate the deeper understandings of the office, the role, and the responsibility of the bishops and specifically of the bishop of Rome. Like the apostles, the bishops are not the successors of Jesus. It is not as if one period of history involves the action of Christ himself and the consequent period of history involves the action of those to whom he has committed the charge of his community of faith. Rather, throughout the long course of Christianity, there is only one who is the Lord of the church, only one who is its master, only one who possesses of himself that authority which governs the Christian community throughout the course of human life: this is

Christ. Those who exercise authority in the church, above all the bishops, do so only as the external manifestation, representation, and instrument of Christ himself, who lives in the church. Thus authority in the church must be exercised according to the manner in which Christ himself exercised it and which he described in saying, "The Laws of the Gentiles dominate their subjects, but this is not so in my kingdom, for I have come not to be served, but to serve, and to give my life for the redemption of many."

This raises, then, the questions: what are the limits of this society, the body of Christ? who are its members? what is the basis of their membership? In this area Catholic theology is presently engaged, as you know, seeking further clarification.

While the church is deeply involved in the mystery of Christ's redeeming and sanctifying action, it does not seem that possession of such sanctification through the grace of God can be the criterion of membership in the body of Christ. Catholic theology would not wish to deny the possibility of possessing essential sanctification in grace to large numbers of sincere human beings who live and die with no awareness of the existence of Christ and who can scarcely, therefore, have part in a community of believers.[21]

The basis of membership in Christ's body would seem to lie, then, more in the area of Christ's priesthood than of his grace. With baptism the Christian is changed interiorly by what Catholic theology calls the sacra-

[21] For a recent official pronouncement in this regard, cf. the letter of Pope Pius XII to Cardinal Cushing in 1949, cited in *The Church Teaches*, 266-280.

mental character of baptism.[22] This change which assimilates the Christian to Christ in his priestly power gives to him the power of effectively entering into priestly action, above all into the sacrifice of the Eucharist. Closely allied with grace, it is not identical with it, and either grace or sacramental character can exist in a person without the other.

If the sacramental character does differentiate baptized from non-baptized, it would be one of the key differences between members of Christ's church and non-members. This would clearly lay emphasis on such membership as an active thing; one would be joined to Christ in the church primarily for the purpose of Eucharistic worship of the Father and for participation in the continuing redemptive work of Christianity.

So much we can say at present, but we await a major theological treatment of priesthood in Christ and in his church. The theologian who provides this need will help immeasurably in the ecumenical conversations which we hope will continue and develop.

[22] Cf. J. Van Camp, "The Sacramental Character: Its Role in the Church," *Theology Digest*, I (1953), 28-31; also the appended bibliography.

SOME FREE CHURCH REMARKS

FRANKLIN H. LITTELL

Some Free Church Remarks on the Concept, The Body of Christ

Some months ago, Professor Paul Minear of Yale published a book entitled *Images of the Church in the New Testament*.[1] In his study he listed and discussed some eighty-eight forms of expression used by New Testament writers in reference to the church. Of these, the references to the image of the "people of God" are the most common (except in the Johannine writings). In the Pauline corpus, the imagery of "the body of Christ"—with body, members, head—is constantly encountered.

In preparation for this discussion I have worked through a considerable volume of notes on the Free Churches and their leaders, in the formative periods of sixteenth-century Anabaptism and seventeenth-century radical Puritanism. I can only report that—for reasons which may be edifying when summarized—they

[1] Philadelphia: Westminster Press, 1960.

greatly preferred to refer to the church as "the people of God," as "a royal priesthood," as "a holy nation," etc., and seemed generally to have shunned the imagery of "the body of Christ." When references are made to the body, the accent is placed upon the common life of the Christians ("members one of another"—I Cor. 12:27, Rom. 12:4-5) or upon the authority of Christ the Head (Eph. 4:15, Col. 1:18). They were plainly opposed to any concept of the church as "an extension of the incarnation." When they used the phrase, they used it metaphorically and not ontologically, as having to do with the structure of the church and not work.[2]

The Restitution of the True Church

To understand what the radical reformation was getting at, we must divest ourselves of the prejudices excited by the polemic of another day and give attention to primary sources. The state-church reformers attacked those they called "Anabaptists" as inspirationists and subverters of the public order. The Roman Catholic apologists considered the "Anabaptists" the logical extreme of Protestant individualism, and agreed in bringing them under the death penalty. The Anabaptists themselves repudiated both individualism and violence and claimed to be restoring the early church

[2] Cf. Ernest Best, *One Body in Christ* (London: S.P.C.K., 1955), p. 195: "The phrase, "the body of Christ", is not, however, used realistically and ontologically but metaphorically in the New Testament. . . ."

in all of her pristine simplicity. They said that all state-churches, whether Catholic or Protestant, belonged to the fallen ("Constantinian") age of the church and that their own movement, marked the beginning of the Restitution. They were, in short, what is technically known as "primitivists." They looked to scripture for guidance in doctrine, church order, and style of life. The plain sense of the texts was to be adopted as normative, without allegory, speculation, or deference to historical development between the time of the "fall of the church" and the Restitution. But more crucial yet, they "opened the Bible in the meeting." That is, the plain sense of the text was to be arrived at in a little church which itself imitated the size, design, pattern of decision, and style of life of the apostolic church.

As a result of all this, they rejected flatly the whole sacramental system as it had developed and the role and status of the clergy which was based upon it. They denied just as vigorously the teaching and style of the Reformers, who objectified the word over against the existing church and built a structure of church-office (*Amt*) and authority founded on preaching. The way in which the Reformers defined the issue then is fairly well known. Said Luther,

. . . the pope attributes more power to the church, which is begotten and born, than to the word, which has begotten, conceived, and borne the church.[3]

Calvin said almost the same thing:

This, then, is the difference between us. They ascribe to the

[3] Hugh T. Kerr, ed., *Compend of Luther's Theology* (Philadelphia: Westminster Press, 1943), p. 137.

church authority independent of the word; we maintain it to be annexed to the word, and inseparable from it.[4]

But this was not where the restitutionists joined issue. They stressed the work of God the Holy Spirit in little meetings, where the word was heard and discussed and acted upon. They believed that the New Testament church unit was the congregation, small enough to make real encounter and "listening to the Spirit" possible.[5] They believed that action—whether in credal statements, matters of church order and discipline, or moral and ethical problems—must express the *consensus fidelium*. They believed that authority centered in the whole believing people, with the universal church represented in a given situation by the congregation—not in a special ruling class set aside either to administer the sacraments or proclaim the word or both.

In the sixteenth century, the Utterite wing of the Anabaptists set aside representative officers—*Diener des Wortes* and *Diener der Nothdurft*—in imitation of the primitive church, while the Dutch Mennonite wing ordained bishops by the same model. Many of the outstanding leaders of the other two sections of the movement, the Swiss Brethren and South German Brethren, were never ordained at all. For Menno Simons (1496-1561) there was a certain rule as to how to know the true church from the pretended church: "namely, where the spirit, word, sacraments, and life of Christ

[4] *Instruction in Faith*, edited by Paul Fuhrmann (Philadelphia: Westminster Press, n. d.), IV:8:13.
[5] Compare statements from the modern science of small group work: cf. J. L. Moreno, ed., *Sociometry Reader* (Glencoe, Ill.: Free Press, 1960), pp. 15-16, 66, 710 *et passim*.

are found. . . ."[6] For Robert Barclay, theologian of the Friends,

. . . it is the life of Christianity, taking place in the heart, that makes a Christian; and so it is a number of such, being alive, joined together in the life of Christianity, that makes a church of Christ.[7]

The "Life of Christianity" was planted in the heart by the Spirit. Writing about the same time as Barclay, John Owen, in a classical statement of the church view of independents, summed up the matter:

. . . as *this whole church-power* is committed unto the whole church by Christ, so all that are committed unto the peculiar exercise of any part of it, by virtue of office-authority, do receive that authority from him by the only way of communication of it—namely, by his word and spirit, through the ministry of the church. . . .

The church is a *voluntary society*. Persons otherwise absolutely free, as unto all the rules, laws and ends of such a society, do of their own wills and free choice coalesce into it. This is the original of churches. . . .

He went on to warn in reference to the celebration of the Lord's supper and other New Testament ordinances "to keep *severely* unto the institution of Christ, as unto the way and manner of their administration" and against "the general introduction of uninstituted rites and ceremonies. . . ."[8] In the Free Church line, the sup-

[6] Section "On the Church" in *The Reply to Gellius Faber* (1554), in *The Complete Writings of Menno Simons* (Scottdale, Penna.: Herald Press, 1956), p. 754.
[7] *An Apology for the True Christian Divinity* (Philadelphia: Friends Book Store, 1908), p. 275.
[8] *The True Nature of a Gospel Church and its Government . . . 1869* (London: James Clarke & Co., 1947), pp. 44-45, 61, 68-69.

per is a memorial and every act of the Christian is sacramental.

I have gone at some length to illustrate the direction of the Free-Church approach for two reasons. First, it is important to note, for the sake of the Catholic-Protestant encounter, that there are two quite different traditions in Protestantism, and the issues which naturally draw the attention of Lutherans and Anglicans and Catholics for fruitful dialogue are different from those which may open unexpected affinities between Mennonites and Baptists and Disciples, and Catholics and Orthodox. Second, and as a consequence, the contribution of the Free Churches to a discussion of the concept of "the mystical body" and its implications for Christology and the sacramental life must, of necessity, be a limited one. When the discussion shifts to the doctrine of the Holy Spirit, they may have a more substantial contribution to make from out of their heritage.

The Case of Menno Simons

The problem can be illustrated in another way. There were two sixteenth-century restitutionists who dealt at some length with the concept of the body of Christ, and both of them accented the distinction between the heavenly flesh and the man Jesus in such a way as to come under the charge of Docetism. The two were Caspar Schwenckfeld, the Christian individualist (*Spiritualist* = spiritualizer), and Menno Simons. Schwenckfeld, in his debates with the Strassburg re-

formers and with the Anabaptist elders, maintained
such an elevated view of the glorious and heavenly
Christ and his church that some said he wouldn't have
been happy even with the church of Jesus and his disciples. Schwenckfeld himself, although little groups of
followers later founded a Schwenckfelder Church (still
extant), decided that the world was so corrupt and the
times so late that no true church (visible) could be
gathered until the Lord Himself should send an angel
with a special commission to that end. In the meantime,
the hidden faithful across the centuries were gathered
up in the (invisible) mystical and heavenly body of
Christ.

The case of Menno is even more illuminating. Menno
was convinced that Christendom, with its mass bap-
tisms and promiscuous "memberships" by whole
populations, represented—whether territorial Catholic
or state-church Protestant—the "fall of the church."
Facing the Reformers, he plainly felt that he and his
people had the better of the argument. He too stressed
the word, and accused them of not following through
consistently what they themselves professed. Like
many a restitutionist to come, he praised the Reformers
for initiating the reform, and then charged them with
being half-way men in not carrying out a "root-and-
branch" reformation along New Testament lines.
When they deferred to the town council in matters of
faith (Zwingli) or retained the medieval parochial and
territorial pattern (Luther), they consigned themselves
to the "fall" and the condemnation of the true head of
the community of the elect. Facing the Catholic party,
he had a great deal more difficulty. He too believed

that the center of authority was the *consensus fidelium*, informed by Holy Scripture and created by the Holy Spirit working in the midst of his people. He believed that the church had both "the key of David," which unlocks the meaning of scripture, and the "keys of Peter," to loose and to bind for all eternity. He believed in a continuing apostolate, carrying all distinguishing gifts of the Spirit. He had, moreover, a strong moral and ethical thrust—including emphasis on the peace testimony and a vigorous *diakonia* among the poor and helpless and diseased—which led reformers like Martin Micron, John a Lasco and Gellius Faber to accuse him of perpetuating monkishness and works-righteousness. He had, however, like some Catholic orders, a strong missionary emphasis—and this at a time when state-church Protestants were agreed that the great commission had been executed and exhausted during the apostolic age and was no longer operative. The line which Menno drew, facing the Catholics, was—apart from the standard charge that they perpetuated rites and ceremonies having no justification according to the norm of the primitive church—precisely in the area which we are discussing.

What troubled Menno was that if the church is in truth an extension of the incarnation, then no criticism of the existing church is possible. He roundly condemned the revolutionaries of Munster for claiming a continuum between their earthly kingdom and the kingdom of God, and he just as vigorously condemned the assertion of a continuum between the heavenly Man and the earthly institution of the church. The church as we know it now is a creature, with a Creator who is also its head. To be sure, the Christians are one in the body of Christ; this, however, has a spiritual meaning and signified the heavenly flesh of Christ:

I say that he is not flesh of our flesh as they have it, but the regenerate are flesh of his flesh as the scripture says.[9]

The question, he said, is which view accords Christ the highest honor. When he went on to spell out, on several occasions, the implications for Christology, he fell into less than felicitous form of words. There were some who felt, even among his own brethren, that in his Christology he severed the nexus in the God-man; and in his ecclesiology he seems sometimes to have two churches, a heavenly and perfect body and a very pedestrian and imperfect association. In any case, it seems to me clear that it was his nervousness before the ecclesiological references to the second person of the Trinity which pushed him to marginal Christological statements. When he was dealing with the church as we know it he vastly preferred to speak of the work of the Holy Spirit, and in this doctrinal area there are riches in his writings which none of the conservative Reformers (with the single exception of Martin Butzer) can match. In this he is, I think, a fairly representative Free Churchman.

In Conclusion

We are discussing the ecclesiological significance of the doctrine of the Second Person, but it is in the un-

[9] Menno Simons, *op. cit.*, p. 772.

derstanding of the work of the Holy Spirit in the church that the classical Free Church tradition has much to contribute in discussions with Catholics (and also the Orthodox).

The Quaker devotion to "the sense of the meeting" is so well known as to hardly require further comment. What is sometimes forgotten is that this practice derived from a style of government of church meetings, back of which lay a whole theology of the way the Spirit brings the claims of the universal church and the universal Christ into focus in a specific local situation. Menno pleaded continually with the theologians of his persecutors to grant him safe conduct for face-to-face discussion and offered to change wherever found in error.

> Then if I err in some things, which by the grace of God I hope is not the case, I pray everyone for the Lord's sake, lest I be put to shame, that if anyone has stronger and more convincing truth he through brotherly exhortation and instruction might assist me. I desire with all my heart to accept it if he is right. Deal with me according to the intention of the spirit and word of Christ.[10]

The devotion of the early men of the Free Churches to the dialogue led to fervent complaints among those accustomed to hearing permanently fixed positions enunciated. Thus Robert Baillie, the Scots Commissioner, complained at the Westminster Assembly of Divines that

> it is not easy to set down with assurance the independent position, both because they have to this day declined to de-

[10] *Ibid.*, in the *Meditation on the Twenty-fifth Psalm* (c. 1537), p. 65.

clare positively their minds, and also because of their principle of mutability, whereby they profess their readiness to
change any of their present tenets.[11]

The independents believed, in short, that there was
sometimes something new to be learned by discussion
which could be learned in no other way. John Robinson's farewell speech to the Pilgrims (nearing Leyden)
is better known than the two previous quotations:

I am verily persuaded the Lord hath more truth yet to break
faith out of his holy word. For my part, I cannot sufficiently
bewail the condition of those reformed churches which are
come to a period, i.e. an end, and will go, at present, no
further than the instruments of their reformation.[12]

That is, revelation was not closed. Speaking as he was
at the very time the Canons of the Synod of Dort were
being defined, Robinson was bewailing the trend in
Protestant scholasticism to fasten upon fixed position,
and anathematize those who dissented or should ever
after change one jot or one tittle of the letter once
formulated and written down.
Although Free-Church men have traditionally hesitated
before the sacramental view of the church, preferring
to emphasize the Third Person rather than the Second
Person of the Trinity in ecclesiological discussions, preferring to urge that the "Church has a more direct connection with redemption than with incarnation,"[13]

[11] Horton Davies, The Worship of the English Puritans (Westminster: Dacre Press, 1948), quotation on p. 243.
[12] Ibid., pp. 200-201.
[13] P. T. Forsyth, The Church and the Sacraments (London: Independent Press, 1942), 2d edition, p. 83. Cf. T. F. Torrance,
Royal Priesthood (Edinburgh: Oliver & Boyd, 1955), quotation

they have also been willing to learn from those who could persuade by the plain meaning of the word and the power of the Spirit. We may hope that this colloquium continue to afford such occasions of grace.

————

on p. 31: "She is not Christ continued, the incarnation continued. One cannot press without interruption from Christ to the church. The cross stands between."

BIOGRAPHICAL NOTES

COLLOQUIUM PARTICIPANTS

REV. ROBERT S. PELTON, C.S.C., is the present head
of the Department of Theology at the University
of Notre Dame. The general chairman of the annual Notre Dame Institutes for Local Religious
Superiors, Father Pelton is also past president of
the Catholic Conference on Inter-American Problems. He has studied at Notre Dame (A.B., 1945),
and the Angelicum in Rome (S.T.L., 1955; S.T.D.,
1955). Among his publications are: *A Thomistic
Conception of the Spirituality of the Catholic
University Lay Student,* and *Spiritual Direction,
A Current Bibliography.* Besides serving as General Editor of the Cardinal O'Hara Series, Father
Pelton has addressed national meetings of the
Catholic Theological Society and the Catholic
College Teachers of Sacred Doctrine.

DR. KRISTER E. SKYDSGAARD, now with the
Lutheran World Federation, is a native of Denmark. He has taught systematic theology at the
University of Copenhagen and has also studied
and taught in Paris, Fribourg, Lukingen, Clervaux
and London. His present appointment as an official observer at the Second Vatican Council at-
tests to his long-time, scholarly interest in the
study of Roman Catholicism. Throughout the
years he has played a prominent role in the work
of the World Council of Churches.

REV. BARNABAS M. AHERN, C.P., is Professor of
New Testament at the Passionist Fathers' Seminary, Louisville, Kentucky. The Scripture Editor

of *Worship,* Father Ahern is also contributing editor of *The Bible Today,* and an editor of the *New Testament Reading Guide* series. His doctoral degree in Sacred Scripture was taken at the Pontifical Biblical Institute in Rome in 1958.

REV. WALTER J. BURGHARDT, S.J., managing editor of *Theological Studies,* also serves as professor of Patrology and Patristic Theology at Woodstock College, Woodstock, Maryland. Recipient of the 1962 Cardinal Spellman Award for Theology that is given annually by the Catholic Theological Society of America, Father Burghardt has written many articles for *America, Catholic Mind, Encyclopaedia Britannica,* and *Theological Studies.* In addition, he is the author of *The Image of God in Man according to Cyril of Alexandria, The Testimony of the Patristic Age concerning Mary's Death,* and *All Lost in Wonder: Sermons on Theology and Life.*

REV. BERNARD COOKE, S.J., is the Chairman of the Theology Department at Marquette University, Milwaukee, Wisconsin. Prior to this, Father Cooke was an instructor in pastoral theology at the Grand Seminaire de Saint Sulpice, Paris. He received his doctorate in Sacred Theology from the Institut Catholique de Paris in 1956. His publications include articles in such journals as *Theological Studies, Theology Digest, Perspectives, Modern Schoolman,* and *Catholic Mind.*

DR. FRANKLIN H. LITTELL, now on the faculty of the Chicago Theological Seminary, was formerly professor of Church History at the Perkins School

of Theology, Southern Methodist University,
Dallas, Texas. After receiving his Ph.D. from
Yale, Dr. Littell took his Doctor of Theology de-
gree at the University of Marburg, Germany. A
consultant on religion and higher education to the
National Conference of Christians and Jews, Dr.
Littell is the author of *The Anabaptist View of the
Church, An Introduction to Sectarian Protes-
tantism, The Free Church, The German Phoenix,*
and *From State Church to Pluralism: A Protestant
Interpretation of Religion in American History.*

Other participants in the 1962 Notre Dame Colloquium
included: Paul G. Barker, Indiana Regional Director of
the National Conference of Christians and Jews, Indianapolis; Dr. John MacKay, retired president of the
Princeton Theological Seminary, Princeton, New Jer-
sey; Dr. Martin E. Marty, Associate Editor of *The
Christian Century* and minister of the Lutheran Church
of the Holy Spirit, Elk Grove, Illinois; Sister Mary Ann
Ida, B.V.M., president of the Mundelein College, Chicago; Rev. George Montague, S.M., Professor of
theology in the graduate school of St. Mary's University, San Antonio, Texas; Dr. Wilhelm Pauck, Professor of Church History at Union Theological Seminary,
New York City; Dr. George N. Shuster, Assistant to
the President of the University of Notre Dame and
former president of Hunter College, New York City;
Dr. Krister Stendahl, the John H. Morison Professor
of New Testament Studies at the Harvard Divinity
School, Cambridge, Mass.; Dr. Leonard Swidler, a
member of the faculty of the history and theology de-

partments at Duquesne University, Pittsburgh, Pa.; Dr. Wilmer A. Cooper, Dean and Associate Professor of Religion at the Earlham School of Religion, Richmond, Indiana; Rev. Charles Corcoran, C.S.C., Professor of Dogmatic Theology at Holy Cross College, Washington, D.C.; Rt. Rev. John P. Craine, D.D., Bishop of the Episcopal Diocese of Indianapolis; Rev. John S. Dunne, C.S.C., Assistant Professor of Theology at the University of Notre Dame; Rev. Mark Egan, O.P., Professor of Dogmatic Theology, Graduate School of Theology, St. Mary's College, Notre Dame, Indiana; Dr. Harold E. Hill, Associate Professor of Old Testament Language and Literature at the Indiana School of Religion, Bloomington, Indiana; Rev. Joseph D. Huntley, D.D., director of educational activities of the Seamen's Church Institute, New York City; Rev. Robert Lechner, C.P.P.S., Professor of Philosophy at St. Charles Seminary, Carthagena, Ohio; and Miss Donna Myers, Secretary of the Colloquium and Associate Director of the Grail Center in Philadelphia. Others who were invited but unable to attend included Daniel Callahan, Associate Editor of *The Commonweal*, Dr. John E. Smith, Chairman of the Philosophy Department at Yale University, and Rev. Alexander Schmemann, St. Vladimir's Orthodox Theological Seminary, Tuckahoe, N.Y.

Some of the preceding also participated in the 1961 Colloquium at Notre Dame. Others who took part in the meeting of that year included: Professor Robert W. Bertram, Chairman of the Department of Religion at Valparaiso University, Valparaiso, Indiana; Rev. Cornelius A. Bouman, Lecturer in the history of the

liturgy at the Catholic University of Nijmegen and a
visiting professor in the Notre Dame Liturgy Pro-
gram; Rev. Francis Cunningham, O.P., Professor of
Dogma at St. Rose Priory, Dubuque, Iowa; Rt. Rev.
Joseph N. Moody, Chairman of the Social Science Di-
vision at Ladycliff College, Highland Falls, New York;
Rt. Rev. Msgr. William R. O'Connor, pastor of St.
John the Evangelist Church in New York City; Philip
J. Scharper, editor of Sheed and Ward, publishers; Dr.
John E. Smith, Chairman of the Philosophy Depart-
ment at Yale University, and Rev. George A. Tavard,
A.A., Chairman of the Department of Theology at
Mount Mercy College, Pittsburgh, Pa.